THE MESSAGES OF
THE LADY OF ALL NATIONS

THE MESSAGES OF
THE LADY OF ALL NATIONS

Edited by Josef Kunzli

Queenship

PUBLISHING COMPANY
P.O Box 42028 Santa Barbara, CA 93140-2028
(800) 647-9882 • (805) 957-4893 • Fax: (805) 957-1631

©1996 Queenship Publishing

Library of Congress Number # 96-70128

Published by:
Queenship Publishing
P.O. Box 42028
Santa Barbara, CA 93140-2028
(800) 647-9882 • (805) 957-4893 • Fax: (805) 957-1631

Printed in the United States of America

ISBN: 1-882972-87-2

PUBLISHER'S NOTE

The *Messages of the Lady of All Nations* presents the words and images that Ida Peerdeman received during the fifty-six apparitions of the Blessed Virgin Mary from the Spring of 1945 to May 31, 1959. Also included are the "Eucharistic Experiences" of the seeress from July, 1958 to May, 1970.

Miss Peerdeman was a modest woman of great integrity. She earned her living as an office worker in an industrial firm in Amsterdam and lived with her sisters. She received her first apparition on the Feast of the Annunciation, March 25, 1945. Her spiritual director, Fr. Frehe, O.P., was present at the time.

The Lady of All Nations declared that the messages were not destined for one country or people alone, but for all the peoples of the world. She gave instructions and advice that all should follow in order to save the world from the power of evil. She taught Ida a simple but powerful prayer and asked that it be spread over the world to prevent further degeneration and destruction.

The *Messages of the Lady of All Nations* also includes important communications, warnings, and prophecies about many topics, such as: the Vatican, different Popes, the Fifth Marian Dogma, specific countries (including America), moral decline, false prophets, disasters, and true peace.

On May 31, 1996, His Excellency Hendrik Bomers, Bishop of Haarlem, gave the *Nihil Obstat* approving devotion to the Lady of All Nations. The Blessed Mother had promised Miss Peerdeman that she would live to see this approval. The approval a reality, Ida, then in her nineties, went to the Lord on June 17, 1996.

On June 7, 1996, Ida had granted Queenship Publishing the rights to publish and distribute the *Messages of the Lady of All Nations* and a second book entitled *Eucharistic Experiences* (describing the visions from 1970 to 1984). Both are available from Queenship Publishing.

IMPORTANT NOTE

The Messages of "the Lady of All Nations" reported in this booklet have been extended by Heaven in a very special way. On May 31, 1958 "the Lady of All Nations" told the seeress: "The contact will remain." Very soon this contact proved to be the Eucharistic Experiences.

These Eucharistic Experiences are dealt with in this present booklet up to and including May 31, 1970. Those received from then to the end of 1984 will be found in the booklet *Eucharistic Experiences*. Then this cycle of Messages is closed.

All of the Messages of the Lady of All Nations, as well as all of the Eucharistic Experiences, were submitted to the Holy Father in Rome through the "Sacristan to the Pope." It is our hope that Rome will soon declare a favourable judgment on the genuineness of these very important apparitions of 'the Lady of All Nations.'

In a smaller booklet entitled *Introduction of the Message of the Lady of All Nation*s some preliminary information on the Messages is provided together with a short explanation of their essential contents. At the same time, attention is drawn to the fact that some important predicted events of the Lady have already proved to come true in every detail. These citations may strengthen every adherent to the Messages in his belief that all other foretold events will be fulfilled with the same convincing evidence in the course of years.

– Josef Kunzli

CONTENTS

EUCHARISTIC EXPERIENCES

INTRODUCTION TO THE MESSAGES

The messages of "the Lady of All Nations" originated in both Holland and Germany. They began in the Spring of 1945, just before the end of the Second World War, and were given to a simple woman who, at the time, was forty years old. She remained unmarried and lived with her sisters in Amsterdam until her death in June, 1996.

All who knew her, honourd and respected her for her modesty and integrity. Decidedly averse to all publicity and sensation, she desired nothing more than to remain unknown. She regarded herself merely as the "instrument" of the Lady who gave her messages so that she might transmit them to the world. When the apparitions began, she was doing office work in an industrial firm in Amsterdam. The apparitions came to her as a complete surprise. As to their character, they belong to the same category as those of Lourdes (1858) and Fatima (1917). They came mostly unannounced and suddenly and, moreover, at various places.

The cycle of apparitions began on March 25, 1945, Feast of the Annunciation, in the home of the seeress. Fr. Frehe, O.P., her spiritual director of long standing, had just arrived on a visit and, thus, he became a witness to the very first apparition. The seeress was drawn to the adjoining room by an inner force. There she saw a brilliant light: a Lady stepped towards her out of this light and spoke to her. To the seeress' question, "Are you Mary?" She replied, "They will call me 'Lady,' 'Mother.'" She also said, "Repeat what I am going to say." Upon this followed a message, which the seeress repeated slowly, word for word, sentence by sentence. It was spoken so slowly that the sister who sat nearby, could easily keep pace while writing it down.

At first, neither Fr. Frehe nor the seeress knew what to do with the messages, which kept coming from time to time in a similar manner.

Later, the messages became clearer. The Lady declared that the messages were not destined for one country or people alone, but for all the peoples of the world.

Up to the year 1970 inclusive, roughly sixty messages were delivered and, in addition, the seeress had a number of Eucharistic Experiences. All the messages the Lady gave were literally repeated by the seeress and simultaneously documented with accuracy by one of the persons present. Afterwards, the seeress supplemented the text by means of explanations.

Two messages were given in a public church, the Church of St. Thomas Aquinas. In all, about twenty Messages, including the prayer, were given in Germany, while the seeress was there on a visit. That this happened by special Providence we learn more than once from the text; for in Germany too, the Lady wanted to give Her messages to the world.

Reading through the Messages, one soon becomes aware that some statements are obscure. Here it is important to remember that most prophetic utterances are obscure. It is only when the time is ripe that the veil is lifted. Even the words of Holy Scripture are sometimes difficult to understand. That was especially the case when they were first told. We need only to recall the words Jesus spoke at Capernaum, concerning the Holy Eucharist. For many they became the occasion for their withdrawal from Jesus, because they no longer understood Him. The Old Testament likewise contains obscure passages. Some of them could be understood only with the coming of Christ. Others again, written for "the latter times," are still waiting fulfillment. – The darkness of faith passes nobody by. That holds good for our times as well. Faith is and remains the touchstone of a true and humble soul.

The Prophecies

The Messages of the years 1945-1951 conceal a number of prophecies regarding the Church, the world and politics. For some souls these prophecies seem too secular. They cannot picture the Mother of God speaking about such matters. Upon a thorough study of the Messages, however, we arrive at a clearer understanding of things. For instance: people today are too much immersed in the world. Their thoughts are much more concerned with the things of this life than the things of the Spirit. However, because the Mother of God has a message for the entire world, She wants, in proof of the genuineness of Her message, to produce evidence for the world, which will make it want to listen. Nobody every listens more attentively than when he hears something about himself. If what is said is accurate, he is compelled to respect what has been said. An example of this is provided by the Samaritan woman, to whom Jesus "told everything she had done."

The prophecies contained in the Messages seem to serve the same purpose. The more they come to pass, the more they gain in importance as a good demonstration of the authenticity of the Messages. At the same time, they promote faith in the reliability and genuineness of the other words and messages.

The Timeliness of the Messages

It is likely that the Lady, by means of the prophecies concerning the future, wishes to emphasize, also, the timeliness of the pastoral and theological messages. For if the prophecies in the secular field already begin to clear and fulfill themselves, then the prophetical messages regarding spiritual things, which form the main contents of the Messages, must be up-to-date and topical as well. That this actually is the case, the Lady makes obvious by means of signs revealing what will happen to the Church. The Messages of "the Lady of All Nations" have been known now for several years. This makes it possible for us to make some sort of judgment of them in depth. They seem, without any doubt, to be directly applicable to our own time.

They have had no ill effects, but on the contrary, they have been a source of inspiration and comfort to many.

Was It Really Mary Who Spoke?

Yet in the eyes of some people the Mother of God used far too many words. They consider it unthinkable that the Blessed Virgin should have spoken so much and repeated some things so many times. They bring to bear the example of other apparitions in which Mary spoke very little or not at all. The answer is this: Mary speaks here in a solicitous manner. She speaks as a mother does when her children are no longer willing to obey. She emphasizes and repeats. She speaks urgently, in an admonishing tone. Mary speaks as a woman, as the Mother of all men. She cannot direct the course of the world and of the Church as She would like to. That is entrusted to man. It is placed into their hands. She respects man's free will. She can only ask and admonish, but She can force nobody. This must be the reason why the decisive parts of the Message are so often repeated. People should impress them on their minds, they should become fully convinced of them.

The Genuineness of the Messages

Fr. Frehe, the spiritual director of the seeress, also had doubts initially as to whether the Messages were really genuine. Accordingly, he asked the seeress to beg the Lady to give a sign or work a miracle. The Lady only replied, "My signs are contained in My words." At the Bishop's instigation, the seeress was subjected to a thorough psychological investigation. This was the report: "This person is perfectly normal. There is not a trace of hysterical propensity. She rather inclines to the opposite, being hard-headed and unimaginative."

As the seeress herself was on occasions thrown into serious doubts and fears, lest she had become the victim of satanic deception, she begged the Lady urgently to give her a sign as a proof of authenticity. This sign followed for her personal information. It was the message of February 19, 1958, predicting that Pius XII would die at the beginning of October, 1958. She received the message for herself alone at three a.m. She wrote it down privately, sealed it and handed it to Fr. Frehe with the direction that it was not allowed to be opened and read before the beginning of

October, 1958. This was observed. Pope Pius XII died quite unexpectedly on October 9th, 1958. He had held audiences up to a few days previously.

The seeress subjected herself constantly and willingly to the authority of Fr. Frehe, her spiritual director, who died in Alkmaar on Feb. 12th, 1967. She obeyed him in preference to the Lady, seeing in him the authority of the Church that had been endowed by the Son of God with the power of the keys. The Lady acknowledges this attitude as correct in the words, "You have acted well. Obedience was your first duty. – So be it! This is what the Lord wanted of you." (Mass of May 31, 1956)

Why were there no visible, public miracles in evidence of authenticity?

To the question why the Lady refrained from public, tangible miracles or sign of evidence of authenticity, as for instance in Lourdes or Fatima, there is no clear answer. But a fitting answer may well be arrived at upon closer scrutiny of our world and time.

Modern man is avidly seeking one sensation after another. Even unimportant, ridiculous incidents are sensationalized. Everything imaginable, including the most intimate and private affairs, are exploited in a sensational way for the sake of business and money. One sensation gives place to another. For most people, this has become a habit. No halt is being made before any taboo; and the most sacred things are thereby trodden under foot.

The Lady did well not to follow in the way of publicity. She Herself said, "In all tranquillity, I have come, in all tranquillity, I shall return to Him who has sent Me." Are these words not convincing and trustworthy enough in the knowledge of the mentality of our times?

Trustworthiness of the Messages

As to the Messages themselves, their genuiness and supernatural origin are especially obvious from the daily happenings in the Church and the world. One may presume with probability that here truly the Mother of God has spoken. A tangible proof of course nobody can produce.* The Messages are spiritual messages. If their fruits are good, one may presume and consider them as coming from God. Another demonstration is not possible, seeing that the purpose and the goal of the Messages are of a spiritual nature. For a scientific demonstration, they offer no basis whatsoever.

The fact that the present book of the *Messages of "the Lady of All Nations"* has received the Church's Imprimatur only means that the Messages are in conformity with the true teaching of Jesus Christ. The Church does not, thereby, wish to express a declaration of genuineness. She merely declares, herewith, that people may read and believe the Messages without harm and that, in fact, the instructions and directions contained in them are useful and conducive to salvation. For their exact observance leads to a complete, living Christianity which fully comprises personal and public life. What would be more desirable for the Church than that this might be realized by all?

Let us hope that the prophecies contained in these Messages may soon work out for the good of mankind. May there be peace and unity among all peoples! The Messages wish to make a decisive contribution towards this promised goal. Therefore, they deserve to be zealously obeyed and quickly spread among all peoples. Peace has its foundation in God alone. The promised "Lady" is granted to announce peace to us. It will really and truly come if we obey Her words.

---

* In these matters, the Church alone is the supreme arbiter. Everything that is written in this book, both with regard to the Messages and otherwise, is submitted completely and utterly to her judgment through the Ecclesiastical authorities.

FIRST APPARITION – 25th MARCH, 1945

I see on my left somebody standing over me in a long white garment, full of womanly grace. I understand Her to be the Blessed Virgin. She lifts up three, then four, and finally five fingers while saying to me, "The 3 stands for March, the 4 for April, and the 5 for May 5th." Then She shows me Her Rosary and says, "This has saved you. *Persevere* to the end (in saying it)." After a brief silence, She adds, "The prayer is to be made known everywhere."

Then in front of me I see nothing but soldiers, many of them Allies and the Blessed Virgin is pointing to them. She takes the crucifix of Her Rosary in Her hand and points at it and then again to the soldiers.

I am given to understand that the Cross must become the support of the lives of those soldiers, for the voice continues, "They will soon go home now – *these here*" and She points to the troops.

I ask, "Are you Mary?"

She smiles and answers, "They will call me 'The Lady' ('Vrouwe') 'Mother.'" The figure walks past me and then I look at the palm of my hand. A Cross is being laid down before me and I have to take it up. I do so very slowly; it is heavy. All at once everything is gone.

SECOND APPARITION – 21st APRIL, 1945

Suddenly, I find myself in a church, the scene is as follows: I am standing in front of a special altar and I see the image of the Lady.

She is standing there surrounded by flowers; they reach right up to the altar steps. Thousands of people are kneeling before Her. The Lady looks at me and moves a warning finger from side to side, saying, "Listen, mankind. You will preserve peace if you believe in Him. Make this known," She adds. This is repeated three times. While speaking, She puts a crucifix in my hand and I have to hold it up in all directions for everyone to see. The Lady points to the crucifix.

After that She takes me outside the church and I sense a great emptiness in front of me. As I am gazing into this void, however, I begin to notice human heads in it. I have to pick one out here and there and the Lady says to me, "These are key people who are even now hatching new plots."

Then I see the Exodus of the Israelites from the land of Egypt and, above them, in the clouds, a representation of God the Father. He is holding His hand over His eyes and the Lady says to me, "Yahweh is ashamed of His people!"

Then I see a vivid representation of Cain and Abel. I can clearly see the ass's jawbone lying in front of me; and then I see Cain taking to flight. After this I am placed again in front of the altar, and in the distance I can see a procession filing past – *the Miracle Procession* of Amsterdam. Then everything disappears.

THIRD APPARITION – 29th July, 1945

I hear the voice again and suddenly I see a sacrifice being offered as in ancient times. The smoke, however, hangs over the altar. I hear the voice say, "Yahweh warns His people." Then I hear, "Be faithful. They have scattered My lambs."

Then the Lady plants a crucifix upon the sacrificial altar and I see, as it were, the whole world gathered around it. The people, however, are standing there with downcast looks and turned away from the Cross.

"Come, My faithful ones!" the voice now calls and I see a chalice being offered to the crowd. "But for a number of them, in vain," I hear the voice say. I feel an impulse to look up and all at once I see the Lady standing before me. She smiles, extends Her arms and calls invitingly. "Come."

A large number of men, of all sorts, is now standing before me: "gentlemen," "rough men" and men dressed in black (priests and religious). Among them all, there is a mixture of good and not so good. The Lady urges them to follow Her, promising to guide them.

Now I see a long and hard road before me, at the end of which there is a great light. "This way," says the Lady, and with an impressive gesture She indicates to the men that they have to walk along this road. The going is very difficult. On both sides, men are falling away. The Lady watches with motherly solicitude and keeps smiling at them compassionately.

Then I see written before me, "Be renewed in Jesus Christ." After this the Lady looks sad and says, "England will find her way back to Me." She pauses and then adds very slowly and quietly, "So will America." Then the Lady slowly disappears and I see a peculiar cloud hanging over the world.

FOURTH APPARITION – 29th AUGUST, 1945

I see the Lady standing before me. She indicates that I should look into my hand – I see strange things coming out of it – I see a great sadness which is put into my hand and I have to look at it. The Lady smiles and says, "But joy will follow." I see bright rays and afterwards large buildings, churches: more and more churches. The Lady says, "They are to form one big Community."

My hand is very sore. Storms are gathering over these churches. Now the Lady is showing *three Popes*. To the left, on high, there is Pius X. Our Pope (Pius XII) is standing in the middle and to the right I see the new Pope.

"These three" says the Lady, pointing to them, "are one era." Then the Lady adds, "This Pope and the new one are the fighters."

Then She refers to a new, yet strange war, in the distant future, which will cause terrible havoc. Much, however, has to be altered in the Church. The formation of the clergy will have to be changed. Now I see lines of young clerics filing past.

"A more modern training is wanted, according to the needs of the times," says the Lady expressly. "Yet good, imbued with the right Spirit.

I suddenly see a dove flying round my hand (still held by the Lady). New rays are going forth from the dove. The Lady then points to the Pope, saying, "Breadth of vision has to come, a more social outlook. There are various movements showing a trend to socialism, which is good, but they should be brought as much as possible under the guidance of the Church."

The Lady looks very sad as She says, "The training of the clergy will have to change in many respects." I can see great counter-currents, much opposition to this in the Church. Then all at once the Lady has gone.

FIFTH APPARITION – 7th OCTOBER, 1945

I see the sun and the half moon; they are standing in the Far East. In China, I see the red flag. After that I see Mahometans and all the Eastern peoples. Above all those nations, I see red on the one hand and black on the other; but there is far less of the black. I hear the voice saying, " It looks as if the latter is dwindling down to a minimum."

Then I see a long and beautiful road. I have to start along that road, but it is as if I have no mind for it. I represent mankind. I set off along the road and I feel so tired; yet I must plod on, very slowly.

I have reached the end of this road, and I am standing in front of a big castle with towers. The gate is opened from the inside. A hand beckons me to come in, but I do not want to (I feel as if I must turn back), yet I go in. Someone seizes me by the hand and I see the figure in white – "the Lady." She smiles at me and says, "Come!" My hand is very sore – it is unbearable – but the Lady clasps it tightly and we go forward. I come into a beautiful garden. She takes me to a certain spot and says, "Here is Justice; those outside (the Lady points beyond the walls) must seek it and recover it or the world will be lost again."

My hand is giving me so much pain, I cannot bear it, but the Lady smiles and pulls me along. We go to another part of the garden and She says, "Here is Truth. Listen well." She continues, moving Her finger to and fro in warning. "Truth, also, is to be found here, but not outside, no, not at all." She says once more.

I want to shake off Her hand. "It is so heavy," I say. But all at once, She points something out to me and it is as if I have a bird's eye view in front of me. I put up two fingers, and suddenly I see our Pope and beneath him the Vatican. Then I see the entire Church of Rome, and in the sky is written, "ENCYCLICAL LETTERS." "That is the right way," the Lady says to me emphatically. "But," She adds sadly, "they are not being lived up to." Once more I see the Vatican and the entire Catholic Church around it. The Lady looks at me and puts a finger to Her lips while She says, "As a secret between you and Me" – and again, She puts a finger to Her lips – "not always there either" She adds very softly. Once more She smiles at me encouragingly and She says, "But it can be righted."

Then I see other churches of various denominations before me. The Lady puts up Her finger in warning and showing me the entire Catholic Church, She says, "The Catholic Church can certainly grow larger, but..."and then She breaks off.

Then I see long lines of priests, students, nuns, etc. walk past me; once more the Lady shakes Her head and, looking severely, She comments, "It is very sad indeed, but all these are unfitted to the task in hand." Then, pointing to the students, priests and other clerics, She adds, "A deeper information is required, one moving with the times, more up-to-date, more social in its outlook." The Lady stresses every word.

Then I see a black dove flying above our Church (not a white one, I repeat, but a black one). The Lady points at the dove, saying, "That is the old spirit, which must give place to the new." Suddenly, I see the black dove changing into a white one.

The Lady then says, "This is a new white dove; it sends out its rays in all directions, for the world is tottering...a few more years and it would perish. Yet, He is coming; He will put the world in order, but..."-the Lady waits awhile – "they must listen." She stresses the word, "must," as if again, giving warning.

Then the Lady continues, "They want to go back, away from here; they do not like to come to this place (castle). Mankind has no appreciation for it."

We continue quite a long way into the garden, until we come in front of a large Cross. "Take it up," the Lady says, "He has gone before you." I refuse and feel as though the people of the whole world did the same and turned their backs upon the Cross. I am pulled by the hand and once more I see the Lady before me, Her hand is in mine. "Come," She says again. I now see a radiant figure in a long garment walking in front of us. He drags a very large Cross, which slithers over the ground. (I can not see His face; it is one blaze of light). He goes on His way with the Cross, but no one follows Him.

"Alone," the Lady says to me. "There He walks, alone in this world. It will get even worse, until the moment when something dreadful will happen and at once the Cross of Christ will stand in the center of the world. Now they must look, whether they like it or not." The I see all sorts of strange figures. Then stars – they also fall, sickles and hammers – everything falls beneath that Cross. Then I see a patch of red. The red however, does not fall away completely.

The Lady says, "All lift up their gaze; they are ready to look up all of a sudden, but at what a cost!..." "It was black on that globe, but now everything has brightened up," the Lady adds, "Now you see that all such things are bound to pass." My hand is getting lighter now.

All at once, I see the Lady again in front of me with the Rosary, and She says, "Keep on praying, all of you." She points to the Cross and says, "The whole world will have to go back to it, great and small, poor and rich – but it will be difficult!"

Now I see the globe before me and placing Her foot on it the Lady says, "I place my foot on the world. I shall help them and lead them to the *proper goal,* but they must listen..."

And then suddenly, everything disappears.

SIXTH APPARITION – 3rd JANUARY, 1946

I hear a voice say, "England, be on your guard!" and I see a large English church in front of me, it seems to be Westminster Abbey. And then I see a bishop. (He does not belong to our Church). Then I see the Pope sitting in front of me and he looks very serious. Once more, I see the same bishop – this has to do with England. I see the word "Struggle" appear. A strange feeling seizes me; it is as though everything within me is changing. I cannot explain how.

I suddenly look up to my left and see the Lady. She is dressed all in white and is in a somewhat elevated position. She points something out to me and as I look, I see England once more before me. The Lady says to me, "There will be a conflict in all Europe and beyond."

A paralyzing feeling takes hold of me. The Lady explains, "It is a heavy spiritual struggle," – "Come." She adds, and points to my hand. A crucifix is placed in it and the Lady shows me what to do: I move my hand with the crucifix all round the globe in such a way that the crucifix *can be seen...*

The Lady says again, "Yes, look at that crucifix." I do so and as I am looking, the crucifix disappears from my hand and I clench my fist. I must look at that too. Then the Lady says, "Now look at the crucifix again." I do so and find it once more in my hand. Then the Lady moves Her finger from side to side in warning and says, "They want to change that cross into other shapes!"

Now I see several things whirling round in front of my eyes, such as communism and a new kind of movement that will arise. It is a combination of the swastika and communism. The Lady speaks again, "The Christians will become *weary* (She stresses the word) of struggling." She points ahead of me and I see a pulpit. It disappears and immediately I see a desert and I hear a call. This is repeated a few times, very quickly. Then the Lady again points something out to me and I see the Vatican. It is as though the latter is spinning round in the midst of the world while the Pope is sitting there with his head erect, two fingers uplifted and looking very intently in front of him. Then I beat my breast three times.

Suddenly, I see someone on horseback, in full armor. I ask who it is and am told, "Jeanne d' Arc" (Joan of Arc). After that, I have to look into my hands and I represent mankind. "They are empty," I tell the Lady. The Lady is watching and then I must join them, while I look up to Her. She smiles at me and it is as though She moves down a step saying, "Come." Then it is as if I am going with Her across the world. Suddenly, I become terribly tired. I tell the Lady, "I am so tired, so hopelessly tired." I feel like that throughout my body.

But the Lady takes me along with Her, always onwards, and then suddenly, I look ahead of me and see the word "Truth" written in very large characters. I read it aloud and then we continue. The Lady shakes Her head and looks very serious and sad and says to me, "Do you see Brotherly Love?" I look into my hands and say, "These hands are empty." The Lady takes me by the hand and again we continue. Then I hear the Lady ask, – while I see before me an endless void – "Righteousness? Justice? Where are they?"

Then I see the Cross once more in the midst of the world and the Lady is pointing to it. I have to carry it, but I turn my head away; it is as if I were mankind and refused the Cross. "No," says the Lady, "it must be carried and placed in the centre; there will be a certain category of people who will fight hard for it and I shall lead them on to that!"

And while She is speaking, a terrible pain seizes my whole body, so that I groan and say to the Lady, "How painful this is!"

After that I hear the word, "Jericho!" being cried aloud, and the Lady, having once more resumed Her position on high, turns Her eyes downwards and, beckoning at me, says, "What I have told you, *must be made known*. If this is not done, there will be no peace."

After that I see the Pope again before me and quite a number of clerics and other gentlemen around him. "It is as if they are in conference," I say. The Lady speaks to me again, "This is the spiritual battle that is being carried on all over the world. It is *much worse* than the actual wars now being waged, because it is undermining mankind."

Then I seem to go across the world and burrow under the ground, and pass through all kinds of passages. It suddenly comes to an end and I hear the words, "Now I am where I wanted to be." Then I hear another voice say, "*Ego sum*," and I add softly, "And the world is small." After this the Lady, with a gesture says, "Go and make the message known."

And suddenly all is gone.

SEVENTH APPARITION – 7th FEBRUARY, 1946

I see the Lady before me. She moves Her finger to and fro in warning and says, "Look across Europe and warn the peoples of Europe." Then the Lady looks very serious while She says, "*Ora et labor*," and again Her finger moves in warning.

Next the Lady lets me see a wolf, which keeps on walking up and down in front of me. Suddenly, the beast disappears and then She lets me see a sheep's head, which has horns around it, as though intertwined. Then the Lady says again, "Europe must be on her guard, warn the peoples of Europe." After this the Lady lets me see Rome; very clearly I see the Vatican rotating. Now the Lady seems to beckon me with Her finger, saying, "Come, look well at that." She holds out three fingers and then the whole hand, i.e. five fingers. She repeats this a few times. "Look carefully and listen," She says, "the East against the West." Then I hear the Lady say again, "Be on your guard, Europe."

Suddenly, I see England before me and the Lady seems to take a step down and to place Her foot on England. I look closely and see the Lady join Her hands and then warn again. I hear Her say, "Woe to you, England!"

The Lady beckons me again to look closely and all at once I see Rome before me again and the Pope seated. The Pope has an open book in his hand, and he shows it to me. I cannot see what kind of book it is. The Pope shows me the book from every angle. All at once, I hear the Lady say, "But much has to be changed there," and She points to where the Pope is. She looks serious and shakes Her head. Again, the Lady holds up three fingers and afterwards five fingers.

I feel confused and hear the Lady say, "Fresh disaster will strike the world."

All at once, I see a plain before me, a large egg is placed on it, and as I watch, I see an ostrich running away swiftly. Then I see lots of black children before me. There is another warning sign and I see white children.

Now I see a scene showing Our Lord standing with children all around. It is a luminous figure that I see. I hear, "Suffer little children to come to Me," and then the words appear, "The children must receive a thorough Christian upbringing."

Next I see a stretch of map before me. I hear, "Judea," and I see written, "Jerusalem."

Then, I see all of a sudden two lines, each with an arrow at the end; on the one it says "Russia" and on the other "America." Then I see the Lady before me and the moon. I say, "There's something getting on to that moon." After this the Lady seems to take me on top of the globe. It is so strange around me and I say, "A kind of phenomenon of nature."

I hear the Lady say, "Peoples of Europe, unite." There is something not in order here. In the middle of Europe, I see Germany and it is as if that country wants to wriggle out of its place.

Then I see England again and I must hold the crown firmly with both hands. It looks as though this crown is toppling. I draw it across that country.

I hear, "England, make *no mistake* as to your task. England, you will have to go back to the Highest, The Highest!" (The last two words were repeated in English.) And now the Lady suddenly disappears.

EIGHTH APPARITION – 25th FEBRUARY, 1946

I see a blazing light and then I see the Lady above me. She points downwards and I see Europe lying before me. The Lady shakes Her head. At Her feet, I see little angels and a while I look at them, they fold their wings over their faces. There is a great light about Her; yet the longer I look at the earth, the darker the latter grows. The Lady draws my attention to this. I look up to Her again, but She points to the earth with a stern look on Her face and there I see in the dark written in large characters, "Truth." All at once, I see the angels again at Her feet and while I look at them, the wings cover their faces once more.

The Lady says to me, "You must warn them; Truth has been lost." I say to myself, "How can I do that?" "Go and spread the message," says the Lady, pointing to the earth below. I can see many clerics and churches there, but only vaguely. With another gesture at the world, the Lady says, "See whether you can find Him," I go about seeking everywhere and finally tell the Lady, "I am so tired and a terrible pain fills me."

Suddenly, I see a large, long Cross coming down from Her and someone is dragging it along. I do not see the person, only the Cross. The Cross follows the long road downwards to the earth, and suddenly I see it standing in the center of the world.

Now I look at the Lady again and suddenly I see a long line of people (I take then to be pilgrims) moving along. The Lady says to me, "Look," and She traces a semicircle, a curve, across the world and it is as though the Lady is writing in it. I read the words aloud. "Truth," this is in the middle. Then She writes a word on the left and I read "Faith"; then on the right I read "Love." The Lady points to it and says, "Go and make it known!" And pointing again to the curve She says, "This will have to come back; to outward appearance it is there, but in reality it is not."

She looks exceedingly sad. After this I have to say, *"Disaster upon disaster, disaster of nature!"*; I see the words "Hunger" and "Political Chaos." *"This applies not only to your country,"* She says, "but to the whole world." I then see the word "Hopeless!"

Suddenly, it grows lighter about me and I see the Lady coming down and She points out to me three words: "Truth," "Faith," and "Love" and She smiles and says to me, "But they have to learn a lot.

She points out to the right and I notice someone with a beard, seated. He holds two fingers joined, pointing upward; under his elbow there is a thick book and in front of him a large key. This scene disappears and the Lady says again, "Look," and shows me something else. It is a large stone and on top of it is a lamb. I suddenly hear the words, *"Ecce Homo."*

NINTH APPARITION – 29th MARCH, 1946

Once more, I see the Lady standing there. She has a child in Her arms. It is as though the Lady suddenly came down and now I see Her standing on the globe. This globe keeps on rotating under Her feet. The Lady looks at me and says, "Come, follow Me."

I follow Her and it is as if we walked over the globe. The Lady turns to me and says, "I want to bring HIM (indicating the child) into this world again." But while speaking thus, She keeps on shaking Her head as if to say, "But they don' t want Him!"

I look at the child and as I look, the child changes into a Cross. All at once, the Cross falls to the ground before me and breaks to pieces. I look at the world and see it is all in darkness. Then I hear the Lady call, "Do bring Him *back* to mankind," and She points to the Cross.

I see the Cross, all at once planted in the middle of the world and around it there are all sorts of people, their heads turned away. I suddenly feel very tired and tell the Lady. But the Lady smiles at me, and suddenly I see Her sitting on a kind of throne. She has the child on Her lap again. The child radiates light in all directions.

The Lady say, "There must be a return to Him *first* of all, before *true* peace can come," and She stresses the word "true." Then words are forming around the Lady, as in a curve. I have to read them aloud: "Truth." "Again!" I say and the Lady nods "Yes." "This is in the middle; I read on the left "Justice," and on the right "Charity." When I read this, I see at Her feet a sort of stone lion, and it is as though it has a halo round its head.

Behind the throne, I see spires and churches appear. I see the Anglican Church very clearly, "With bishops, not of our Church," I say, and while watching, I see an X-cross forming through it and the Lady smiles. The child on Her lap has suddenly grown up; it stand upright now and has a chalice in its hand. Then I see a ladder appear beside all this, and it is as though I mount it.

I reach the top of the ladder and suddenly see another sign – an X with a P across it.

The Lady say, "Religion will have a hard struggle and they want to tread it under foot. This will be done so cunningly that scarcely anyone will notice it. But I give warning," and She looks very serious and points to the chalice. Suddenly I hear Her say, "Christus Regnum."

After that I see Jerusalem lying before me. There is a fight and all of a sudden I see Armenian priests in front of me. Then I hold up two fingers. Again, I see the Lady seated on Her throne with all the above-mentioned things around Her and now I see the Anglican Church, a Russian Church, an Armenian Church and many more besides. They are spinning round together. At this, the lady looks worried and I hear Her say, "Rome, be on the alert!" She stresses these words and clenches Her fist. All of a sudden, the Lady is gone.

TENTH APPARITION – 9th JUNE, 1946

Once again the Lady stands before me. She shakes a warning finger and She seems to say to the world, "*Urbi et Orbi, that* is for the moment the most important thing." The Lady comes down and She carries a little child with Her in a shawl. She indicates that I should follow Her and I walk behind Her. The Lady sets down the child in the midst of the world and the child begins weeping aloud. The Lady points to the child and says, "Let those who are for HIM, be watchful! I cannot give sufficient warning." Then again I look at the place where the child is and He has suddenly disappeared. The lady looks sadly on mankind and says very dejectedly, "Righteousness, Truth and Love are not to be found among men." After that the Lady, gazing intently in front of Her, says, "*Disaster upon disaster!* For a second time I tell you: as long as these are missing, there can be no true peace."

Then the Lady says, "By praying and not only by *praying,* but especially by *working* for the right end...Work and watch!" Then I notice that the Lady has stepped aside, and from the other directions *demons* are coming towards me.

I hear the Lady say, "I predict another great catastrophe for the world." This She says very sadly and She keeps on making gestures of warning. She continues, "If people would only listen!" and She keeps shaking Her head -but they will not!" Then I sense a short span of time and hear, "Apparently, things will go well for a short time." I see the globe and the Lady points to it and it looks as though the globe will burst asunder on all sides. Then the Lady points at the sky. She stands to my right, in the West, and She points to the East. – I see a great number of stars in the air. "That is where it comes from," She says.

Suddenly I see a Cardinal's hat lying before me and above it an X-sign appears. There will be a struggle in Rome against the Pope. I see many bishops and I hear a voice say, "Catastrophic!" Then the Lady disappears.

ELEVENTH APPARITION – 4th JANUARY, 1947

I see the Lady, She says, "Let them look for support in *the only* Truth!" She lets me feel the world with my hands, and I feel a very severe pain. The Lady says, "This is the world at the moment." Then, again, I touch the world with my hand and the Lady says, "This is the world of later; it is very, very heavy. The world will destroy itself."

Then the Lady takes the globe in Her hand and rotates it. She says, "It has to improve again, but!..." and I look where the Lady is pointing to and see several Churches and in the midst of them Rome. The Lady says, "Rome, be forewarned!"

Then I see the Anglican Church, and I notice a change coming about. The Lady comes a step nearer and says, "Look," and now I see a number of church-towers closely packed. Round them the

Lady puts an iron hoop. Together we look at it and the Lady says, three times in succession, "Up higher!"

Then She starts writing above the church and I read aloud, "Brotherly Love." This She puts in the middle above the towers. She writes on the right, a little lower down, "Justice." She goes to the left and writes, "Truth." In the meantime, I hear the Lady say, "All this has *not yet* come about. How often have I said this?" And She shakes Her head compassionately.

All of a sudden, I see Rome and the Lady point to it and says, "I cannot give sufficient warning that they should practice this in the *fullest sense.*" Then I see great changes which the Lady shows me.

Now I see as follows: huge red waves which penetrate more and more deeply. I see them going farther and farther and I hear the Lady say, "This is good, but...more spiritual, *genuinely* in Truth, Justice and Love! Then it looks as if – years ahead – I see quite different spiritual trends. The Lady says, "Once again I warn Rome. They have to take a broadminded view; but!" And while the Lady again points to the words She has written, everything suddenly disappears.

TWELFTH APPARITION – 30th AUGUST, 1947

I hear the voice, I look and I feel a sense of heaviness weighing me down. I hear the words, "There is a great pressure" and I see Italy before me clearly. A heavy thunderstorm seems about to break over it. I have to listen and hear a voice saying, "Exile." I pass as it were above Italy, and it is as if I must deal blows. Then, again, I hear a voice say, "It seems to be raining blows!

In the meantime, I see the North of Italy and the southernmost point very clearly; while what lies in between seems to be dead. Then I see a great dome arise, and very heavy drops of rain begin to fall over the church or dome. It is no ordinary rain, but drops of blood. In the distance I see a Cross standing in the light and I hear: "There will develop a great politico-Christian struggle – politics within the Church" Then I see a great hall in the Vatican and there is the Pope seated. Something seems to be going on in the Vatican. Time and time again, secret meetings are held. They assemble in secret. It seems to me that an ambassador from America is among them also. In front of the Pope, there are all sorts of papers. The Pope is kept informed about everything. He is completely aware of what is happening. There is so called peace, but not a true one, all pretense before the world. Then twice, I had to rub one hand over the other and I hear: "That will happen twice." And then I see a point of time.

THIRTEENTH APPARITION – 7th DECEMBER, 1947

I see the Lady and hear, "Rome is in danger!" After that a big "4" appears before me and round it a circle. That vision vanishes and then a large Cross appears before me with four equal beams. Around that too, a circle appears and in the middle of the Cross I read "I.H.S." This I take up and show it around me and now I notice crowds of people standing about us, and they are looking at it; but many with repugnance.

Then I see heavy, thick clouds appearing above Europe and *huge waves* engulfing Europe. I see the Lady standing in a glaring, bright light. She is dressed in white. She keeps Her arms extended and from Her hands flow a thick beam of rays. I have to hold up my hand and then it seems as if the shaft of rays is put in my hand. I feel it burning and smarting. The Lady smiles at me and points to my hand, while She nods Her head in assent (I do not know what this means).

Then the Lady's face becomes very sad and drawn and She points to the heavy, lowering clouds and huge waves. She says, "They will first have to perish by the flood and only then..." and I see the words written down and after "only then," appears the word "all..."

Then the Lady's face brightens and I see *the water* going up in the form of vapor, and the sun seems to shine through it for awhile.

The Lady directs my gaze to the earth and I notice that the water has all evaporated, and I see bones scattered over the ground and I hear the Lady say: "This is the desolation. But go and work, work!"

Then She points upwards and says: "Read," and I see letters appear and I read: "Righteousness." I feel an excruciating pain in my hand, and it feels as heavy as lead. Once again, I hear the Lady say, "Come, read further," and I see in massive letters before me "Brotherly Love" and above that I see icicles forming with drops of water dripping from them. I hear the voice again, "Read once more," but though I want to read, I cannot, for there are flames playing around the letters. For a moment, the flames rise and I read "Justice."

Then I see numerous crosses in rows as they are over the graves of soldiers in a cemetery. One after another, they tumble down, falling backwards. Once again the Lady points and I see new white crosses appearing. For yards and yards, as far as I can see, they rise out of the ground. I hear the Lady say, "This is my message for you today," and then the Lady disappears and I feel an emptiness about me and all is dreary.

FOURTEENTH APPARITION – 26th DECEMBER, 1947

Suddenly, I see a bright light and I feel a pain arising in my hand – but it is only a beam of rays. I see the Lady and She says, "Disasters *will overtake the world* – from North to South, from South to West and from West to East."

Now I see a round dome. It seems to be situated in Jerusalem and I hear, "In and around Jerusalem, heavy battles will be waged." All at once, I see Cairo clearly and the sight fills me with a strange sensation. Then I see various eastern tribes – Persians, Arabs, and so on.

The Lady speaks again, "The world is as it were going to be torn in two," and I see the world lying before me and a great rent appears diagonally across it. Black clouds are hanging over it, and I feel great sorrow and misery.

I hear the Lady say, "Great misery and distress are imminent." Then I see an Eastern region with white-roofed houses. I feel something heavy in my hand and while I look, a crucifix is put in it. I have to set it down on the ground. It is heavy and sways continually in all directions – backward and forward and from side to side. For a moment it looks as though it would fall forward, but then it straightens up and seem to be lighter now and firmly rooted in the earth. I feel compelled to look at the ground and I see bones and helmets lying under the Cross. A large key appears in my hand, I let it fall; at once it lands among the bones and helmets.

I now see lines of young men marching past me, they are soldiers. I hear the voice say, "Give our young men the spiritual help they need." Then I see white graves appearing, small white crosses everywhere.

A pain develops in my hand and I see America and Europe lying side by side. After this I see written: "Economic warfare, boycottings, currency crises, catastrophes."

Then I see a number of figures whirling and intermingling with one another. First of all, I make out torches, which cast their light in three directions – West, North and East. Then I see blue and white stripes intermingling and then stars. After that I see the sickle and hammer, but the hammer breaks away from the sickle and then all things whirl around together. Then I see the crescent and the sun; these too commingle with the rest. And, finally, a sort of buck or mountain goat comes jumping through the lot. While all this is whirling around together, a circle appears on the left and through this the Globe is turning. Now a big pointer appears and I hear the words. "The hand of the sun-dial is going in the opposite direction!" This picture too disappears. Now I see something like a cigar or a torpedo flying past me so rapidly that I can scarcely discern it. Its colour seems to be that of aluminium. All of a sudden, I see it burst open. I feel with my hand and have a number of indefinable sensations. The first is a total loss of sensibility. I live and yet I do not live.

Then I see faces before me (swollen faces) covered with dreadful ulcers, as it were a kind of leprosy. Then I am aware of terrible diseases (cholera and so on).

Then tiny little black things are floating around me: I cannot distinguish them with my eyes and it is as if I were made to look at them through something (a microscope) and now I see (what the seeress now knows to be) slides of extraordinary brilliancy and upon them those little things enlarged. I do not know how I am to interpret this. "Bacilli?" I ask. The Lady says, "It is hellish!"

I feel my face swelling and it is swollen when I touch it, all bloated and quite stiff. I can no longer move. Then I hear the Lady again, saying, "Just think! This is what they are preparing!" and then very softly, "Russia, but the others as well." Finally, the Lady says, "Nations, be warned." – and now the Lady disappears.

FIFTEENTH APPARITION – 28th MARCH, 1948

I see the Lady and She says, "The rights of man will be the point at issue. Within a short time, tremendous things are going to happen. They will be preceded by chaos, confusion, doubt, disorder and despair. Above St. Peter's, heavy clouds will hang, which will only be dispersed with much strife and difficulty." She stresses, "Failure to do this would mean ruin."

"All Christians must unite in solidarity. This will only be effected with great pain and misery. Unite, all of you, for the struggle begins. The gates are opening. The Eastern peoples are holding their hands before their faces in Jerusalem. They will weep and wail with great anguish over their city. There is a large well in which you all can wash yourselves. Until these words have found full acceptance in men's minds and hearts, there will be no peace in sight." I see written: "Righteousness, Love and Justice."

Then I see a Cross planted in the ground. A snake wriggles up on it; all round me it grows dark and dreary. I see a sword hanging over Europe and the East. From the West, a light is coming. Then I hear the Lady speak again, *Christian peoples, the heathens will teach you.*

Next I see the Pope surrounded by a reinforced bodyguard. I hear the Lady say, "Boobytraps!" Black clouds are hovering above St. Peter's. Then the Lady says, "Be just and act up to your teaching. Cover your eyes with your hands and enter into yourselves."

A Cross is placed in my hands and it hurts. It is so heavy that I can scarcely keep my hold on it. "Grip it tightly" the Lady says. Great rays of light stream forth from it. And suddenly, the Lady and the light have gone.

SIXTEENTH APPARITION – 7th MAY, 1949

I have to hold up two fingers and then I see a Bishop in full pontificals. Next I see a stone catafalque with a high dignitary of the Church lying upon it. On top is a Cardinal's hat and above that a sword and a crown in oblique position.

Then a large gate is opened before me. I have to enter. Somebody in a long gown is standing before this gate. I shudder at the thought of crossing the threshold. Now, of a sudden, I see the Lady and She says, "Be brave and go in."

When I have entered, I see a big, circular room. "This is a dark area," says the Lady. "you must penetrate very deeply into it. This is the depth and the darkness of the times."

Suddenly, I see the Lady sitting in front of me, clad in mourning with a white veil draped over Her head. She looks very old. She sits stooped. The Lady says, "We are here in the darkness; it is the *degeneration* in mankind."

Then I see a crucifix before me and the body slides down from it, so that the wood is left bare. "*The way of the Cross begins anew*" the Lady says.

I see deep furrows in Her face and big tears running down Her cheeks. Now I go with Her more deeply into the darkness. Our walk seems to last for ever, and I see nothing but darkness. "Oh, what is that?" I ask. We enter a cave. The Lady lets me feel the stone (natural stone). Then a little straw is put in it and a child is placed on the straw. From all around, people are streaming in. "Ordinary people, the least of my children," the Lady says. There is no room for them elsewhere – whole crowds of them!" "The least of My children," She keeps repeating.

Suddenly, before my eyes, the place changes into a church – an endless number of churches. In that church, there is straw and a baby lying on it. Now the Lady takes me along with Her through all those churches and points out to me the empty pews.

She says, "Do you see the mistake that has been made? – Nobody there!" – And then white cards (like name plates) appear on all the pews. "Do you see the mistake?" the Lady asks again. Then She stretches out Her hand over those plates and I see that the pews are all bare- the plates have disappeared.

"The least of My children!" the voice says again: and it is as though She is trying to fill up these pews with people. Then I see a Bishop. The Lady says, "Point it out to him" and She indicates the churches. She continues, "The world, but above all the Church, must be detached from everything!"

Then I see St. Peter's and the Pope sitting there with his head bowed, his bodyguard around him. All that, too, is placed in the grotto. Next the Lady writes a large "P" with an "X" across it. This She puts down at his feet and in front of it, the Cross is placed, the long beam pointing upwards, (thus upside down) and the Lady says, *"Where are your soldiers?"*

The Pope sits with his fingers raised and above his head is written: "VIOLENCE." Ever more violence! Then I see soldiers standing behind the Pope – they are wearing a peculiar kind of "helmet" and holding up two fingers. The Lady says, "Then a great battle will begin in the world"; and I see two powers opposing each other. Suddenly, I see a large field of waving corn; it is waving very slowly. Then I hear the Lady say, "Degeneration!" She repeats it once.

The Lady then says, "Russia will try to deceive everyone in everything she does. There will be a complete revolution" and I see the globe, as it were, rotate once. Then the Lady says, "Nature, too, will change!"

I hear the words: "Christ is gone." I go about seeking and I hear, "Realism, spirit of realism." I also see this spirit in some way or other. Then we arrive inside the grotto again and all the fruits and riches of the earth are being brought and placed in it. "And now," says the Lady, *"We are going to share out. This was the spirit they have not understood."* Next the Lady shows me a bare Cross and lays it down flat. I see something quite new, namely a central area, very blue and unending in depth. Round about it are beautifully coloured spheres. Then I feel myself being pulled, as if by a kind of magnet. "These are forces of nature," the Lady says. "you will hear of them."

We continue on our way until suddenly, we are in the light. I find myself in another sphere. Here my hands become very heavy and numb. Within this sphere, terrible, nasty pains come at me from every side. There is the bright sphere.

Suddenly, I see St. Peter's again and next to it the Anglican Church, an Armenian Church and the Russian Church, with a band encircling them all. The Pope is sitting at the head, holding the two ends. In the background the word "Atheists" rings out. They form a semicircle around it and around that another curve appears. Thus, the Church is surrounded. I hear the Lady say, "In this way, we are not able to save her." Then I see an ass with people taking flight. (A woman with a child sits on the ass' back – an Eastern scene).

I see before me Europe and next to it America. I seize something from the middle of North American and from it I sprinkle – *what* I do not know – over Europe. In the distance I see a multitude of Eastern peoples. "These he will rouse," says the Lady. I see all this very far away. Then a skull appears and I hear the Lady say, " *A great disaster will occur; that will startle them.* The Baltic is full. You do not see that."

Now I have to trace a line from North to West and so obliquely down. I do not know what this signifies. Then the Lady says, " They are looking for peace, but it is not to be found." And the Lady leaves.

SEVENTEENTH APPARITION – 1st OCTOBER, 1949

I see the Lady. She says, "My child, I will help you; have confidence, even in difficult moments." She puts a Cross into my hand, it is so heavy! She says, "Child, this is the Cross you will carry with you."

Now I see written before me: "1950" and then "1951-1953." I see St. Peter's in front of me; drops are falling upon it – tears or rain. Then the Lady says, "*Do give warning that as things are now, we are not getting anywhere.* My Son is being persecuted again. Take the Cross and be sure to plant it in the center. Only then will there be peace."

Then, suddenly, I see the Balkans. There is a war; they are fighting again. The Lady says, "Child, there will be a fierce struggle. We have not seen the end of this struggle yet. *Economic disasters* will come. The empire of England is tottering." And now I see a rope attached to the crown; they are pulling it in order to keep the crown in balance. Then I see the Pope and a Patriarch.

Then the Lady says, "Come along to Russia." I see all kinds of people in glass buildings, underground as well; there seem to be Germans, Frenchmen, Poles, etc, among them. "They are making chemicals. America, be warned!" – "*Intervene, do intervene,*" says the Lady, and then. " It is not human lives alone that are involved here, but higher power. You must bring the Faith back into the world again. But the faithful...? "and the Lady shakes Her head. "Do live according to the Faith – *Brotherly Love*. For it is Love that is the First Commandment! Righteousness comes next."

Now I travel with the Lady down the Danube, and She points all around Her and says, "Work is to be done here, work is to be done there." She points, from left to right. "It must be brought again *to God*. The people are ready for it, but their leaders are unwilling."

And then all of a sudden, the Lady is gone.

EIGHTEENTH APPARITION 19th NOVEMBER, 1949

The Lady is there again. She shows me Italy, saying, "Here those in authority must work. Mere *words* avail nothing. What is wanted is *deeds*." Then it is as though St. Peter's is rocking. The Lady says, "In Italy more must be done against Communism. Do warn Germany and Italy, they can be saved yet. You must tell them to work against the *degeneration* of Germany. The people are good, but they are the prey of circumstances. We must bring the Cross there again and place it is the center. Beginning with youth, they must work up the Faith and instill it again. Unless hard work is done in Italy, it will perish, the least of My children must be roused."

Then the Lady, as it were, takes a great crowd of people to a certain spot and, whilst I look on, I see the Lady pushing these people to an altar, on which there is a large crucifix. The Lady says, "This is the work the *great* ones of this world should be doing, but..."She moves Her finger to and fro and shakes Her head – "But no!"

"Therefore, we must work together. Do tell them that." The Lady says. "They must pray still more. Pray to ward off this *degeneration*. The whole world will destroy itself, if this is neglected. That is why I showed you this."

And in a flash the Lady is gone.

NINETEENTH APPARITION – 3rd DECEMBER, 1949

I see the Lady standing there and She says, "Child, I will give you another message for Germany. It *must* be saved!" Then the Lady takes me, as it were, over Germany and shows me the conditions. She says, "Let the Bishops work! They must get their priests to work especially amongst the young, against humanism – modern paganism."

In front of me, I see a host of crosses. The Lady shows me how those are being taken to various places. Then, I see a large Square in Berlin (where the Reichstag-building is). The Lady seems to plant a large Cross there, saying to me, "People must be led to that. Youth must be kept away from paganism. They must do *their utmost* to achieve this."

Then I see Rome. The Lady moves Her finger to and fro in warning and says, "Oh! Oh! Why do they not start right here? A radical change is necessary." It is as though Her hand turns everything upside down.

Next She says, *"Holland, too, starts sliding down."* I see young people and the Lady says, "They stand on a downward slope." Now She takes me somewhere. In front of me, I see two very high mountains and between them a very deep and dark chasm. It seems as though I am placed on one of those mountains. The Lady says, "Look..." and I see an abyss in the middle of the earth. Suddenly, the Lady seems to bring the two mountains together, saying, "This chasm must be closed."

Then I see St. Peter's. The Lady says, "Child, there you see the Pope in full pontificals. He holds up two fingers." She continues, "Listen well, the *doctrine is correct,* but the Pope is *right* in changing the *laws.* He must not relax his efforts."

I see the Pope still sitting before me, holding up two fingers. Now I see a large council hall, in which the Pope is seated. "Child," says the Lady again, "The laws may be changed, some can and other *must* be changed. The various social classes must be brought closer together. Let Rome carry it through and set an example to the whole world. Do think about this and urge it. And again I tell you: "Love is the *First Commandment* and next to it, as if linked to it by a bracket, are Truth and Justice." "Child," says the Lady again, "look." And I see a "50" standing between the Lady and the Pope. Then She says, " In that year hard work will have to be done and...not only in words. The doctrine of Christ is *correct*, then why is it not being *lived correctly* and in all its refinement?" Then I see around me little dots and in the center a big, red one. The Lady presses Her hand heavily upon the red one, saying, "This is the main thing; people do not live up to this very well; a radical change is necessary. If they do not take these warnings to heart, they will perish and end up there." Then, I see again those mountains with the chasm.

Once more, I see the Pope and the Lady says, "He has but to *command and it will happen*." Then I see Italy and strange clergymen of high rank: Cardinals, Bishops, and so forth. They are gathered in a large council hall, and it is as though *the Pope is drawing up a decree*. Then, again, I see a link between the upper and lower classes. "That is what we must strive after," the Lady says. "Never forget Love and Righteousness. Let all who believe, work together *for the good.*" I ask, "*But are you really the Lady?*" She looks at me with a smile and says, "Ask your director to believe you; he has sufficient evidence. Tell him this: his intentions are good and he loves his *work*; for the rest..." – The Lady makes a movement with Her head and hand, adding, "For the rest, he need not worry. This is simply the way his life has been directed. The evidence has been given for both of your benefit. More I cannot say, as yet. It will become clear *over* the years. Tell him this." And then the Lady leaves.

TWENTIETH APPARITION – 16th DECEMBER, 1949

I hear the Lady say, while with a stern look She moves Her finger to and fro in warning, "Poor, poor Germany! Do take up the Cross of Christ and plant it in the center. Rouse the Clergy; start with the least. The working classes must be brought again to *Him*. You must realize that *this* is the way the other one works," and the Lady clenches Her fist and shows it to me.

Then I see St. Peter's; the Lady stretches Her hand over it and says, "This *must* and *shall* be protected. The other spirit is infiltrating with such dreadful success." Then before my eyes I see a great mingling of white and red clouds. It is as though they move quickly alongside and through one another. Beneath the clouds I see silhouettes of several church-towers and domes mixed together. The Lady shows me this picture, and then, as it were, disentangles the clouds with Her hands, I see a very dark-blue area and in its center a bright light. It is like a very bright star, flashing before my eyes. The Lady touches the light with Her forefinger, very gently, yet so powerfully, that I can hear the impact as though She struck with a hammer. She says, "Here they must land!"

Then I see heavy clouds before – very black ones – and the dome of St. Peter's. Next I hear the voice say again, *"There will be a battle, it will be heavy and it will flare up suddenly.* We have a long way to go yet."

Now I see the Pope sitting in front of me. The Lady looks very serious, turns Her head sideways and says, "The Church must be urged on. *Urging people on is not enough;* they must act in the true Christian spirit. You think that all this (teaching) is of value, but it must be translated into deeds. I hope I have made myself sufficiently *clear.* There must be still more hammering upon social justice, righteousness and brotherly love, but...by means of acts; not with words, but with deeds. Deeds can bring them to the light that I have shown you."

Then I see Europe before me. The Lady says, "Europe take warning, *unite in the good cause.* This is not merely an economic warfare: the aim is to corrupt *the spirit.* It is a politico-Christian warfare. Those at the top must give the lead. They have to set an example; I have, alas! also to remind the clergy. They must make contact with the least of My children."

Then I see above the Pope and St. Peter's written in large letters: "Brotherly Love," "Righteousness." The Lady resumes, "The lack of these is the great fault of this time. Unless these are lived in practice, things will steadily grow worse and the world will sink lower and lower. Each one must make it his own concern to live up to these." Now it is as though the Lady places a Cross in my hand, saying, (while pointing to herself) *"Not Me, but the Cross!"* Then it is though She makes me read a blackboard on which is written: 50 – 51 - 53, and She says, *"During this period there will be warfare and disaster."*

She extends a hand in protection above the dome and with the other She covers Her eyes. I get a fearful, burning pain in my hand. "I cannot bear it," I say.

Then the Lady says, "The spirit will keep on trying to penetrate in every possible way, slowly, insidiously. It will proceed in such a subtle way that the nations will not recognize it. Again, I warn you to pass this on."

Then I see Italy. There I see an ordinary, simple man, a priest. He seems to be standing in the midst of a large crown, preaching. With a smile, the Lady points to him, saying "That Father Lombardi is doing a good job. He works along lines such as We *desire."*

After this I see two rows of different churches before me. The Lady seems to walk towards the front row and lightly pass Her hand over it. The churches fall en masse and disappear. Then the Lady, drawing a rhombic frame for me, says, "Child, this is the center." Now I see a dome and around it a wall in the form She drew it. That dome is St. Peter's. A narrow stream runs round it, bordered with a thin, black line. Again the Lady says, "This is the center," and the Lady's fingers move to and fro very slowly, very heavily. " Let that *remain the center!* The minds of this world are intent on destroying *the center.* I will help you."

Now I notice that the Lady again holds Her hand above the Pope and St. Peter's. On my left, I suddenly see a big black paw. The paw seems to claw through all this.

What a pain is now gripping me. Everything is turning pink and red before my eyes. Whilst that paw sweeps about, I see ahead of me a black eagle, in full flight, going to the left.

I see Germany on my right. I hear the Lady say, "Take heed, Germany!" I see a triangle drawn over Germany and the Lady says, "The spirit of the triangle tries to enter under a different form. The people are good, but they are pulled hither and thither and find no way out. Poor Germany! They *will be* and *are* the dupe of that other big one."

Then I suddenly see a German Bishop before me in full pontificals. He is an elderly man, a strong figure. On my right, a layman appears, likewise a strong, manly figure. I hear, "The bishops under *His* jurisdiction and then somebody comes from the other jurisdiction. But that is for later on. (The latter one). Germany will attempt to extricate herself. Italy also." Then again I see that simple priest surrounded by people. "He is trying to get the *truth* among people," says the Lady. Addressing me, She adds, "You must make this known. Do tell them."

And all at once the Lady is gone.

TWENTY-FIRST APPARITION – 14th FEBRUARY, 1950

I see the Lady who says to me, "My child, I have come to tell you what my message is: work is to be done and hard work, too!" Then the Lady moves Her hands, as though beckoning several people to come and stand before Her. She says, "I do not see them yet, the armies of young men and girls. Why is it not set on foot and why is it being neglected?" And the Lady seems to look around for them. She adds, "That is why I have come to draw attention to it. This is meant for Germany too."

The Lady continues, "There is a strong tendency in the world towards what is good and this is just why the *other spirit* is at work. That spirit is busy influencing and corrupting the world. Mankind is not bad in itself, but weak." Then, again, the Lady seems to hold a crucifix in Her hand and put it on a kind of dais, saying "Do you see that crucifix? To this mankind will have to be led back. I ask them urgently, in this modern world with its modern technology, not to forget that simple Cross."

After this I see the Pope before me and round him the whole Vatican. The Lady seems suddenly to be standing above it all. And I see, so to speak, big drops falling on the Vatican, drops coming from the Lady's direction. The Lady, giving warning, again says, "The Church is still given the chance now; more I will not say about it. I spoke of the modern world. Why does Rome not look for *still more* modern means and why do they not work in a more up to date way? They should take advantage of *these* means to win the mind of the world. There will be others to cater to the body. The Church must influence *the mind*. This is a most opportune moment; for mankind is seeking. The attack is no longer directed against nations, but against *the mind* of man."

The Lady continues, "There will be a great struggle- America and Russia – that is coming." Then I feel an excruciating pain in my hands.

The Lady says, "Japan will be converted." I do not know what that means. I sense a terrible pain coming over India. The Lady lets me feel it in my hand.

Then She says, "If Rome works hard, much more progress will be made in all directions."

Then I see the Vatican. The Lady, again, is standing on top of it and She moves Her hands as though placing several churches round the Vatican. The Lady says, as if speaking to herself, "*Now* there is still a chance," and adds, "This Pope must realize what an enormous task he has to accomplish at this present time."

Now She shows me Germany and says, " Do ask that the Pope send directives, for Germany has so great a need of the *right Spirit* and it is *through these* that it can receive it." I see an Archbishop in Germany, a sturdy figure. "He will be at the head of the struggle," I hear the Lady say. Then She makes a zig-zag line with two fingers wide apart, right across Germany, and says, "Do work upon the young people in Germany – all you that have been appointed for that. I am not telling you this for nothing."

And then the Lady leaves.

TWENTY-SECOND APPARITION – 27th MAY, 1950

I see the Lady standing there and, looking at Her hands, She says to me, "Child, I still see empty hands. I ask you to pass on that it is really my firm determination to form a group from among that core of people that *want* the good and that *do* good. Listen well, much time is spent on material things; let them also give their time to the spiritual! It is very necessary. I should like that club of people to realize this. Once again, I warn you: Catholics must work hard; a great danger is threatening. Italy will be torn in two." Now, the Lady shows me St. Peter's again and says, "The *opposite* camp too is working to form as great a center as this. Hard work must be done in Germany. Fortunately, a start has already been made for renewed and better work among the faithful. But, that is not enough by any means. Germany, above all, must be very alert. There is a double game being played with Germany."

Now I see a very large group of young people standing round the Lady. She looks and points at them, saying, "Child, oh let them begin!" – and with another gesture at the group- "Get the young people back into the *right* religious frame of mind. It is hard and difficult for those who have that at heart. However, I cannot insist upon it enough. It is high time to begin now."

"This is for later on," the Lady says, *making a kind of curve with Her hand*. I do not know how this is to be interpreted. Then the Lady resumes, "You will see that the Cross will be set up again, *only after much misery and disaster.* Let each one do all that he can. Once more I point out to you that the first and great commandment is "Love," "Brotherly Love.""

And now the Lady is suddenly gone.

TWENTY-THIRD APPARITION – 15th AUGUST, 1950

I see somebody making the following gesture three times: crossing the arms over each other, palms downwards. After that the arms are slowly moved apart and then crossed as before with the palms pointing upwards. Then I see various symbols, such as little curves, dashes and dots. Then I see a kind of letter, something like our 'J,' then again various separate signs.

Now I see a wall, bending and twisting. It seems as if it were coming down a mountain. This gives me an excruciating pain. Then I suddenly see a beast before me (a symbolic beast). After that I see lobsters and big starfish. Next I see the outline of an island. It seems to be Formosa. A smaller island lies farther down. Then I have to push something away to the left, and make a swooping movement over the island. Now I hear the words, "America, be forewarned here." After this I have to fold my hands and look above to the left.

I see the Lady and hear Her say, " This is the age of politico-Christian warfare. I have already said this several times." Then the Lady says, *"Great events are now coming to a climax.* The chaos I spoke of has set in. Disasters have come. Some governments have already resigned and *more will follow.* Note well, my child, the fight is about to begin. I show you these four fingers and draw a circle round them. A monarch will reign, very briefly and powerfully. You will not see it in your own restricted circle."

The Lady resumes, "Look," and suddenly a few beasts place themselves before Her. "Look," She says again, and I see a wolf standing before Her on Her left. Then a wolf or dog, holding a torch in its mouth, comes and stands straight in front of Her. Beside it is a lioness. And on the extreme right appears a large falcon or eagle.

"Look," the Lady says again and now She points upwards and I see a white dove. The Lady says, "This is the *new spirit* that is to come." And, then, I suddenly see rays issuing from the dove – two rays downwards, two rays to the right, and two rays to the left. The Lady says, *"You will understand the meaning of this later."* As I look at that group (the Lady with the beasts and the dove), it all becomes surrounded by stars.

After that the Lady seems to take a step down and She says, "Come," and now we arrive at a kind of plateau and stop in the middle of it. "Do you see this?" asks the Lady, pointing from East to West. She now stretches out Her arms and seems to place two walls opposite each other on the plateau. They stretch away out the distance.

Suddenly, the Lady stands above it and says to me, "That is no good." She points to East and West. Then She spreads Her hands and clenches Her fist. After that She says, "Listen carefully and clench your fist and strike as often as I do." I clench my fists like Her, and the Lady counts while we strike our fists forcefully together. "Three times altogether," says the Lady. "Half of this, is the East."

Then I see the Balkans and Greece surrounded by a big chain; East Germany is inside, also. The Lady seems to tie all these countries up with the chain. I notice that one part is still free and in the background I discern a sitting figure leaning his head on his hand. The voice says to me again, "These are the people that plan and bring about destruction to the world."

After that I am shown an Eastern scene. We climb the mountain once more and on the top is again the plateau. On it we stand still. The Lady points to something lying on the ground. "Come," She says, and points to the ground. I see a heavy beam and have to push it away from me. Then, suddenly, I see a cross-beam being added to it and together they form a Cross.

I look again at the Lady and say, "What am I to call you?" (I had to ask this again) She answers me. "Just call me, *The Lady*."

The Lady, indicating the beam pushed away, says, "Christendom," and She makes a movement with Her hands and fingers, as if demonstrating that everything was breaking to bits and fluttering about. After that She says, "Pass this on: Christendom, you do not know the great danger you are in. There is a spirit that is out to undermine you, but"...(and Her hands make a sign of blessing), "the Victory is Ours."

The Lady continues, "I will take you with Me and show you," Now I see England lying before me. The Lady places Her foot on England and, moving Her finger to and fro in warning, She says, "Why so slow to change? Can you not turn to what is normal?"

Then She places a very big crown on England, saying, "This, also, will be tampered with." She seems to make little holes in the crown all around, through which She pulls tapes. Now She seems to fasten all these tapes to England. Then Her foot is withdrawn from England. The Lady says, "No, England, these are not the right politics." I suddenly see the King before me; he seems to turn round. This happens very quickly. Above England, at an angle, I see Churchill – but only his head. Then the Lady points somebody out to me and I see all at once a bishop, but not of our Church.

It seems to be the Archbishop of Canterbury. The Lady is looking at him and She moves Her finger to and fro. I see a great number of spires appearing in the background. The Lady continues, "There a change is ahead." (But I think She meant later).

I see the Pope on our left. He has two fingers uplifted. On the other side, facing the Pope, stands the Archbishop of Canterbury, who is suddenly joined by another clergyman. The latter seems to be wearing a white gown with white bands. Then I see the Lady, standing over the heads of the others. The Lady says, "Watch" and She moves Her finger all over the heads of the English clergyman and then sticks it between the Pope's uplifted fingers (forcing it through). This comes from the side of the English clergymen.

Then the scene disappears.

Now I see written 51, 53. The Lady shows me this and unexpectedly I get something into my hand. It seems as though I have to snatch it from the sky. It comes from very high up. I hear the voice say again. "These are meteors, watch out for them!" Then the Lady says, "Come" and we go on.

Again, the Lady speaks: "The fighting in Korea is an omen and the beginning of great distress." Then I see *demarcation* and intervals being marked out. Next I see someone leaning his head on his hand, in deep thought. I take him to be Stalin. "I have warned you against that danger," I suddenly hear beside me.

Then I see one hemisphere of the globe. I have to look over it. And whilst I hold the left-hand corner with my hands, I have to say, "Here I look very far down and I hold it tight." I have to descend at an angle to the right and go straight on. This gives me terrible anxiety, "We shall continue," says the Lady.

Then I see the northern part of Italy and have to grasp it in the palm of my hand. After that I see Southern Italy and I take hold of the "heel" with my thumb, whilst the other four fingers are placed on the rest of it. I am compelled to do this.

I hear the Lady say, "No, things are not in order at all there. Where are the Encyclicals?" I have to make a movement and cross my hands with the fingers pointing upwards. Then I keep on seeing empty hands.

Next I see St. Peter's and hear the Lady say, "Do you know your power at all? Do you know your teaching?" Then once again the Lady writes "Encyclical" and She says, "All right then, see that they are carried out. Let their teaching spread to the left and to the right, to the top and to the bottom. Do you realize (and She clenches Her fist) *how powerful this* force is?"

Next She lets me see a 1 and a 2 and a 3. After that I see a book. A hand is laid on it. The Lady says again, "Look to your laws," and She seems to stretch something every longer and wider. While doing this, She says. "Know well that your time has come."

After this She takes me on to a slope and says, "*Urbi et Orbi*" Then we both look from that slope at St. Peter's, "Why so narrow? Why not more widely extended?"

Then She takes me into a space between and says, "This is where we must get to." I feel a kind of oppression and I hear, "From all this chaos a struggle will first ensue, and only later there will be an ascent."

All at once, a sadness envelops me and the Lady departs, saying, "I shall come back and give you messages again.."

TWENTY-FOURTH APPARITION
16th NOVEMBER, 1950

I see the Lady standing on the globe. She points at the globe and says to me, "My child, I am standing on this globe, because I want to be called 'the Lady of All Nations.'" The words 'of All Nations' arrange themselves round Her in a semicircle. The Lady goes on to say, "I have told you: Mission work at home – and *now* I want to show you something." Then the Lady points at the globe and is now standing on Germany with Her two feet tightly together. She moves one foot and places it on England, and says, "I have already placed My foot there."

Then She withdraws Her foot to Germany and presses both feet firmly together again. She is standing with hands outspread, looking down upon Germany very dejectedly, and says, "My child, I have placed both My feet upon Germany. This country must be saved! The Son has just brought you here (Germany) in order that you may grasp this more readily. I have restored the health of many sick people.

She now points to the map and I see Lourdes and other places. "Do you understand now what I want here? There are so many sick *souls* here and they must be saved. Why do so many priests from Germany go to the Foreign Missions? Let them stay here, where so much work is to be done!"

Then the Lady points and I see the Vatican, while She says, "Let the Pope send the means and encourage vocations, otherwise Germany will perish. There is a terrible falling away from the Faith. The people do not want to make offerings for new churches and buildings. The priests must be urged on to play their part. It is a heavy task. I am only warning. The others are hard at work to draw the German people away from Rome."

Then, all at once, I see a skull with cross-bones before me. The Lady takes these and lays them at Her feet upon Germany. "The Son wants to give His special protection and has sent Me to help Germany. But they must be urged on to *those things* I have pointed out," She says.

Then I see many little children gathering round Her, looking up to Her as though in ecstasy. The Lady points to the children and then on my left I see men and women standing at a great distance from the Lady and the children. The Lady brings Her hands together and says, "Germany must start to regain unity. Let a beginning be made by everyone for himself in his own home. The children must be reunited with father and mother. Let them kneel down together again and say the Rosary!"

Then the Lady seems to disperse the children and She explains, "Make it a habit at home, and then it will spread into the world. Brotherly Love must be practiced more again. There must be a great drive among the Catholics. This can be advanced through propaganda and more preaching about it in the churches. Altogether, there must be more action. (And all the while it seems as though the Lady pushes the people forward.)

"It is of great importance that this is carried through. There are others at work to destroy Germany. The people are now prepared. Do tell them." And the Lady makes a warning gesture with Her fingers, saying, "Let them work hard!"

After that I see the Pope before me and the Lady says, "The Pope will see to this, if it is asked of him."

Then the Lady extends Her hands crosswise over Germany and steps off Germany and I see the globe turning under Her feet. Then I see Her again standing on the globe and She points to Rome. She moves a warning finger to and fro, saying, "Let the Pope *continue in this way!* Now there is a great chance for Rome." I see different churches before me and the Lady, with one hand as it were, throws these churches to the ground. In the background, I see the great dome of the Vatican. And the Lady says, "The great opportunity has come *now, provided that the Pope carries out* what he intends to do." She stretches out Her hand in protection over the Pope. Then She says, "A great disturbance will be experienced all over the world. The Russians will not leave things the way they are at present; and therefore, I say, 'I am 'the Lady of All Nations.'"

TWENTY-FIFTH APPARITION – 10th DECEMBER, 1950

I see a light approaching from the left. I have to fold my hands. Then, suddenly, I see the Lady standing on the globe again. After that it seems as if the Lady took me along and now I see Her spreading out the globe before me like a flat map. Then She places something on the map and at the same time a terrible pain comes over me. I see that the Lady has laid a very massive Cross on top of the map. While I look at it, I get a fearful pain in my hands and head. It feels as if all the muscles were contracting. The Lady, pointing to the long beam, says, "This is the beam that is being laid upon the world." Then She points to the cross-beam and finally to the whole Cross, saying, " I shall let you feel the pains of that beam." A feverish sensation comes over my head and I get a violent thirst. The Lady makes me put up two fingers and the thumb of my right hand. The left I have to clench. Then the Lady says, "The right hand is the Truth and the other the fist, which you have to hold up high so that all the people can see it." Whilst I do so, I suddenly see a large variety of people from all nations appear, standing behind the globe with the Cross. Now I have to hold my fist before my eyes. At that, a terrible pain seizes me, which causes me to writhe and begin to cry. "That fist is so very painful," I say.

Then I fold my hands anew and the Lady says, "Come, we will stop in the middle of it. I will set my foot down in the midst of the world and show you: that is America," and then, She immediately points to another part, saying *Manchuria – there will be tremendous insurrections."* I see Chinese marching, and a line which they are crossing.

Then I have to move my hand up and down over Formosa and Korea. I hear the Lady say again, "My child, I told you that it was an omen. By this I meant to say that there would be periods of apparent tranquillity, which, however, do not last. The Eastern nations have been roused by an ideology that does not believe in the Son." We continue on. Now I see China Proper lying before me. I have to fold my arms in a peculiar manner and suddenly I see a great man, sitting on a throne and the Lady says, "He is troubled. His empire will be divided up for the time being."

Then the Lady points out America and moves a disapproving finger to and fro, as She says, "Do not push your politics too far."

After that She lets me run my hand twice over the Cross, which weighs heavily over America also.

I see Asia. The Lady seems to spread Her hands over a certain part of it – to my mind the Ukraine – as if in protection.

Then up, to the left, in Russia, I see a hellish light. It seems to explode from the ground upwards. "And then you see nothing anymore," prompts the Lady. And now I see a plain burnt out.

In front of me I see people with hands crossed over their chests, shawls upon their heads and wide cloaks draped around their bodies. The Lady points to them, saying, "There too will be a war

again for *holy ground* and they will fight a battle for Our places."
(The last part I did not hear very clearly).

"Japan too, must be on her guard. I am telling you *all* this, for
you will live to see it. After that, *I am 'the Lady of All Nations' and
you will proclaim that."* Then the Lady stands in from of me again
in Her usual attitude, with outspread hands. And I ask Her, "Will
they believe me?" The Lady answers, "Yes, this is why I came
before, when you as yet did not understand it. Neither was it necessary then; it was to serve as evidence for now."

I have to clench the fingers of one hand again and raise the
other, the fingers pointing upwards. The Lady then says, "These
two hands will fight against each other, but after much strife and
pain the hand with the fist will fall; for the Truth will always triumph. But alas! much will have to be changed yet. Make known
that the Church is now on the right path."

The Lady waits a little, before She adds, *"The secular and regular clergy!"* And then the Lady strikes the table with Her fist and
shakes Her head in an emphatic "NO!" while She says, "In the
case of the seculars – they should be so much more committed!
Let them take their calling seriously in this present time!"

Then it seems as if the Lady is re-arranging people in two rows.
Now I see to Her right men standing and to Her left women. With
a compassionate look on Her face, She points to the women, shakes
Her head and says, (as though addressing them), "Are you yet conscious of your role? Listen well: as woman is, so is man. You,
women, must set the example. Come back to *your womanliness."*

Now the Lady looks at the men and says, "I have one ques-
tions for you, men: where are the soldiers of Christ? More I
need not say."

Then it seems as if the Lady is uniting the two rows of people.
She brings them together by means of a curve. Now I see unending
rows of men and woman standing next to each other. Then the
curve becomes a large dome and above that dome something like a
big church gradually forming. In the middle of the church, a representation appears. It is a white dove, emitting rays of light. The
Lady says, "Oh, let these come upon the people of the earth! *I will
help them,* but they will have to work hard and quickly!"

I suddenly see the Pope again, but only from the shoulders upwards. He stands as it were above it all. He is wearing a peculiar crown all set with precious stones. While I am looking at it, I hear the words, "A tiara." Then the Lady addresses the Pope, saying, *"You are going in the right direction, I will help you.* Use your modern means *still more* and persevere. The chance for Rome has come; do make use of it! You will have to weather *very severe storms*, but you will be protected."

Then, suddenly, I see a crown in the right hand of the Lady and it looks as though the Lady is offering it to the Pope. The Lady speaks to me again. "Now we move on. France is in a very sad plight." I see France and in the middle of it the picture of Napoleon. Then I hear, "France, you have fallen off badly, in the military, economic and spiritual sense. Where are your glory and your pride!" I see many red spots over France and I hear the voice say, "And yet so very little would be necessary to make these people see the error of their ways."

Then the Lady points to various countries and says, "Tell me, *why do they not unite?"* I see the Netherlands, France, Belgium and England. The Lady indicates a thick line on Germany, saying, "Europe has been split in two." I erase that line at one sweep. And now I see nothing but a black area except for the coastal regions, which I see very clearly. I hear, "The Oder." And suddenly I see it flowing. "It is red with blood," adds the voice. I see red branches going westwards. Now I hear, "Turkey, are you on the alert?" and I see the Bosporus and the Dardanelles.

Now the Lady bids me make a gesture – fasten both hands on the map like claws and I hold my arms as though they were paws. The Lady says, "You only represent that," and She explains, "You are as a beast that stands with two paws upon Europe, ready to pounce." That beast looks to the right and looks to the left. I draw back the paws very slowly and I hear the voice say, "After agonies and pain you will finally see the following": I suddenly see before me a peaceful landscape, with *lambs and sheep at* pasture and a shepherd in their midst. Then the Lady say, *"Be sure to grasp all this and make it known."*

All at once the Lady is gone.

TWENTY- SIXTH APPARITION – 25th JANUARY, 1951

"In the night between January 24th and 25th, 1951, I dreamt that I was standing in a peculiar hall or room somewhere far away. There all at once, the Lady stood opposite me. She had a large cloak thrown round Her shoulders, a scarf or shawl on Her head and sandals on Her feet. She said to me, "Look well and listen."

I saw before me a long table and behind it a kind of couch, on which several men sat down, half reclining. In the middle, I saw a luminous figure with bread in front of him and a chalice of wine. The Lady stood behind it all and said to me once more, "Look well and listen." And suddenly the hall turned into a big church full of people, in the middle of which the Lady and I stood watching. Next I heard the Lady's voice, saying, "A *decree* shall and *must* be issued, ordaining that the people need no longer have been fasting before going to Communion. There are so many people who, just when they are in church, feel a tremendous need to go to Communion, and are debarred from it because they have not been fasting."

Then the Lady pointed to the men and said, "These men also went to Communion straight from the street." (and in a flash I saw that room again). "Look," the Lady said, "at first few people go to the Communion rails." And then I heard a voice as if it came *from outside* and issued that decree, and now I saw the people streaming to the Communion rails. "Like this it must and shall be," the Lady said. "Do you see the difference now?" and immediately all was gone and I awoke.

TWENTY-SEVENTH APPARITION
SUNDAY, 11th FEBRUARY, 1951

I see a bright light and then I see the Lady standing there. She says, "I am the Lady – Mary – Mother of *All* Nations. You may say, 'The Lady of all Nations' or 'Mother of All Nations,' who once was Mary. I have come precisely today in order to tell you that I wish to be known as this. Let all the children of men, of all the countries in the world – be *one!*"

Now the Lady remains standing silently in Her usual posture and keeps on looking at me. Then she speaks again, "The whole world is in revolution, but the worst is that mankind itself is revolutionized. – Come with Me." Then it seems as though the Lady walks over the globe, rotating it. Now I suddenly find myself standing above Italy. I see the Vatican and right in the middle of it I see the Pope. He has the tiara on his head, a scepter in one hand, and holds the other in the well-known attitude, with two fingers raised. All around him I see cardinals and bishops. Then I hear the Lady say to me, "Look carefully, these are the bishops of all countries."

All at once, the Pope has a large book in front of him and the Lady says, "Listen well, My child. Some changes have already been made and others are under discussion. I, however, will deliver the message of the Son: the doctrine is correct, but the *laws* can and must be changed. I have come to tell you this on this particular day, for the world is being revolutionized, in which direction, nobody knows. That is why the Son desires me to have this message handed on."

And now I am suddenly standing in front of a large Cross, looking at it. I am seized with terrible pains. It is as if the muscles of both my arms contract, so that my fingers clench.

Next, my head seems to split asunder and I feel as though in a fever. All this together makes me weep. I can bear it no longer and ask the Lady whether it might pass. It lasts for another moment, and then everything is gone again.

Then the Lady says to me, "Let all men return to the Cross! Only this can bring peace and tranquillity." I am still standing in front of the Cross with the Lady. She says to me, "Repeat this after me. Do say this prayer in front of the Cross":

"Lord Jesus Christ, Son of the Father,
send now Your Spirit over the earth.
Let the Holy Spirit live in the hearts of all nations,
that they may be preserved
from degeneration, disasters and war.
May the Lady of All Nations, who once was Mary,
be our Advocate, Amen."

I am still standing in front of the Cross and have said the prayer and repeated the Lady's words phrase by phrase. Now I see them written in large characters.

The Lady continues, "My child, this prayer is so short and simple that each one can say it in his own tongue, before his own crucifix; and those who have no crucifix, repeat it to themselves. This is the message which I have come to give you today, for I have *now* come to tell you that I *want* to *save* the souls. Let all men co-operate in this great work for the world! If only everybody tried to follow this for himself!"

Then the Lady lifts a finger and adds, "Especially as regards the first and great commandment – Love." Now I see the word written in large letters.

"Let them begin with that!" She says. "The little ones of this world will say, 'How can we begin with it? Is it not the important people who do this to us?' and I tell the little ones, 'If you practice Love in all its refinement among yourselves, the big ones will no longer have a chance to harm you. Go to the crucifix and say the prayer I have taught you and the Son will grant your request.'"

Then the Lady speaks to me again, "Another great catastrophe of nature will take place. The great ones of this world will never come to an agreement. Men will be seeking, turning *this way* and *that*. Remember the false prophets. Seek and ask only for the true Holy Spirit. There is, at the moment, a war of ideas. It is no longer races and nations that are at issue; the fight is for the spirit. Have no doubt about this."

Then the Lady folds Her hands and I see the Pope surrounded by cardinals and bishops. She says, as if speaking to the Pope, "You can save this world. I have said it more than once. Rome has its opportunity. Seize the present moment. No Church in the world is constituted like yours."

"But do move with the times and urge your up-to-date changes on religious, priests, seminarians, and all the others. Keep an eye on that and carry it out to the smallest detail. The doctrine must remain intact, but the laws may be changed. Let the children of this world benefit more by *'The Remembrance of my Son.'*"

Then the Lady turned to me saying, "I have shown you in a dream how the practice of frequent Communion can be achieved. This holds good for the Netherlands, as well as for all the countries where it does not exist. For Germany, I have this message: 'Let them work assiduously in that country to bring the people, who have strayed very far, back to the center of man's life. – THE CROSS! – There is a shortage of priests, but of lay people there is no shortage. Let a great movement among the laity be organized to gain them for the campaign. Carry out this work, above all, with great love and charity. Let the great ones in Germany give their help and not turn away from the Church.' (She speaks in German):

"'*Deutschland jedoch liegt mir sehr am Herzen. Die Muttergottes weint uber die Kinder Deutschlands.*' (I am greatly concerned about Germany. The Mother of God weeps for the children of Germany).

"To France, Belgium, the Balkans and Austria, I say: 'Do not let your *mind* be formed *in the wrong way.*'

"To Italy I say: 'Great ones of Italy, do you realize what it is you have to do?'

"To England I say; '*I shall return, England.*'

"To America I say: 'Do not push your politics too far; seek after the truth.' I am glad that America is better disposed to the Faith at the moment.

"For Africa I say: 'Let it be known that I desire a seminary there. I shall assist the Dominicans. Tell this to your spiritual director. Tell him also that the Son is content with his work and guidance. Tell him that he should discharge his responsibility in these matters with greater courage. I only want to make use of you to carry out the will of the Son in *these times*. Indeed, I also wish to ask you that you, child of man, should help mankind as much as you can. I shall give you the necessary strength and support.

"Your director has been chosen to help you precisely in this work. The rest can remain as it is. He will understand what I mean.' In addition, I wish to say to the Eastern and Asiatic peoples, whether they know the Son or not: We are concerned for them."

The Lady points to the globe and says, "*This time is Our time. You, child, are the instrument chosen, so that you may pass on these things. You shall do it. There is plenty of evidence even in what I have told you this very day. Tell them that I wish to be 'The Lady of All Nations.'*"

TWENTY-EIGHT APPARITION – 4th MARCH, 1951

I see a bright light and then I hear the words, "I am here once more." Through the bright light I see the Lady. She says, "Look carefully. Listen to what I have to tell you." Then the Lady shakes Her head disapprovingly and says, "Child, you will hand on my message, won' t you? My sole purpose is to ensure that the Will of the Son is obeyed in these times. Understand well, you are only the instrument." After this I see the Lady standing clearly before me and She says, *"Look at My picture and study it well."* Then the Lady lets me look carefully at Her and even feel with my hands the contours of Her figure, from head to foot. Then She says, "Now, imprint this clearly on your memory: I am standing on the globe and both My feet are firmly fixed upon it. You can also see clearly My hands, My face, My hair, and My veil. The rest is as though in a haze. Look closely at what protrudes from both sides of My shoulders and above my head." I say to the Lady, "That is a Cross; I can see the cross-beams and the upright protruding."

"Then," says the Lady, "you have seen everything well, haven' t you? I have shown you My head, My hands, and My feet like those of a human being – mark well: like those of the Son of Man! All the rest is Spirit. *Have this picture of Me painted and together with it, spread the prayer I have taught you.* This is My wish for today. And I want this to be done in many languages. *This is the reply you should give to your director."*

"Child," says the Lady again, "once more I insist that this must be done. It is of great importance, that you, human being that you are, do not allow yourself to be deterred from it by others. You must be brave and see it through."

Now I ask the Lady, "I feel so weak in the face of such a task. Will they believe me?" The Lady answers, "All I am asking you is to do what I say. More is not expected. I have no other desire, but this. A mere human creature like you can not understand what great value all this can have. Tell your director this as well. In these days, I want to be 'the Lady of All Nations' and, therefore, I require of you to get the prayer translated into all the principal languages and said every day. *Fear nothing."*

Now the Lady stand motionless in front of me and I have a clear view of Her. Then She says, "Now I will explain to you why I have come in this way: I am the Lady standing in front of the Cross. My head, hands and feet are like those of a human being. The trunk, however, belongs to the Spirit because the Son came through the Will of the Father. Now, however, the Spirit is to descend upon the world and this is why I want people to pray for His coming." Then the Lady pauses before she adds, " I am standing upon the globe because this message concerns the *whole world.*"

Then the Lady seems to draw a semi-circle with Her hand, while She says, "Look closely." Now I see a semi-circle stretching from one cross-beam to the other. The semi-circle seems to consist of a peculiar light and in it I see appear letters printed in black. On the left side I see the words, "The Lady"; in the middle above the head, "I have My special reasons for giving you this here (in Germany). What they are, you will learn later. You have My message of today. Pass on everything with great care. The spirit of untruth is making such appalling progress, that it is necessary to act quickly. The whole world is degenerating, and for this reason the Son sends 'the Lady of All Nations, who once was Mary.'"

TWENTY-NINTH APPARITION – 28th MARCH, 1951

I see a bright light and then I hear the words, "Once more I am here – 'the Lady of All Nations.'" Then I see the Lady standing before me clearly. She says, "I have come solely to give you the message: tell your director that at the moment things are going well. Nevertheless, the Son demands *obedience*. His will must be carried out. Examine carefully, once more, what I look like."

Now the Lady comes closer and again she shows me everything clearly. Then She says, "This is how it will have to be made known. In the text of the prayer I taught you: 'Lord Jesus Christ,' etc. *nothing* is to be altered."

And, again, the Lady says the prayer for me and lets me read it in printed letters.

I notice that the little word "now" in the phrase, "Send now your Spirit" as well as the word "All" in "The Lady of All Nations" – is underlined. Then She says, "The words 'Who once was

Mary,' must *remain as they are*. Further, tell your director that prudence has its place, but the Son has sent Me to carry this out – such is His Will. Do not be afraid, child. I stand before the Cross as *The Lady* and thus I wish to be brought back to the world. And you, my child, are the instrument, merely the instrument. Some time ago, I showed you these dates: 51-53. Do you know, child, what kind of period this is? It is a time such as the world has not experienced in centuries – such falling away from the Faith! and therefore I desire that this should be done, swiftly and fearlessly. Tell your director; in these modern times, in this modern world, which knows so well how to act promptly and swiftly in material affairs, it is equally necessary, in spiritual matters, to act swiftly and without delay."

Then I suddenly see Rome before me, and the Lady, passing Her finger back and forth in disapproval, says, "Do you know your laws?"

Then the Lady speaks to me again, "Tell your director not to be afraid. He will understand Me. It is Me who has chosen him and you to pass on my words. Today, My special message is that there should be action. I have told you earlier on, that the Cross must be brought back into the world – in these years – 51-53. You do not know what the future holds. You have no idea of the great danger Rome is in. Rome still thinks itself to stand securely; it is not conscious of *how* it is being undermined! Do you realize that theology must yield to the interests of My Son? – I shall move from the Cross and stand beside it."

Now the Lady steps aside and it seems as though I was placed in front of the big Cross. Again, I am in the throes of those excruciating pains. This only lasts for a short while, and then the Lady takes Her stand again before the Cross. "My child," She says, "you will do what I ask, won' t you? I will assist you and the others.

I desire that it should be spread in many languages. In this work, I will help them. Do not be so frightened. Why be afraid of things which are coming from the Son? Make this devotion known. Otherwise, the world will degenerate completely. Otherwise, there will be war upon war and no end to destruction.

Rome must be conscious of its role in these days. Does Rome know who the enemy is that is lying in wait for her, like a serpent stealthily making its way in the world? I am not referring to

Communism alone; there are yet other "prophets" to come, *false prophets!*

Therefore, it is absolutely necessary that you make use of all these means. I stand as the Lady before the Cross, as the Mother before My Son, who came through the Father in Me.

This is why I stand before my Son, as the Advocate and as bearer of this message to this modern world."

THIRTIETH APPARITION – 1st APRIL, 1951

I see a bright light and I hear a voice say, "My child, last time I came only to let you know that it was I." And now suddenly, I see the Lady emerging from the bright light. The Lady says to me, *"This time* I have come to give you further explanation. Look closely and listen carefully to what I have to tell you. I stand here and I wish to be 'the Lady of All Nations' – not of one special nation, but of all. Listen carefully to the explanation I am about to give, and try to grasp the contents of this message. I stand before the Cross with My head, hands and feet as those of a human being. The rest is of the Spirit. Why do I stand like this? My body has been taken up like the Son was. Now I stand an oblation before the Cross. For I have suffered with My Son, *spiritually* and above all – *bodily*. This *will become a much contested dogma."*

(I tell Her that I am anxious about this message).

Then the Lady says, "My child, do pass it on and say, 'This brings the Marian dogmas to a conclusion.' You have nothing else to do, but to hand this on. I have said that theology must yield to the interests of My Son. By this I mean: theologians, the Son always uses what is little and simple for the carrying out of His designs. Do you have the same simple faith that you are trying to inculcate in others? *Childlike faith.* We cannot afford to let time slip by idly. This time in Our time."

Now the Lady, without a word, remains standing before me for a long time, looking at me with a smile. Then She moves away from the Cross and again those grievous pains beset me. First all, the muscles of my body contract in a terrible cramp. When this fades away, I feel spiritually very strange and tired. Then, suddenly, I see the Lady again standing in front of the Cross and the pains stop. Now I see the Lady as if through a haze, standing in front of the Cross, whilst, looking through Her body, I can see the Cross clearly.

Then of a sudden those terrible pains begin anew. They last but for a minute and then everything goes back to normal and the Lady says to me, "My child, just as He suffered, so did I suffer as the Mother of the Son of Man. Repeat this correctly." then the Lady draws my attention to the globe on which She is standing. Snow is falling all around Her. She smiles and says, "Don' t you understand? Look closely at the globe."

And now I see the globe deep in snow. The Lady, smiling again, says, "Have another look at the globe." The snow is now melting into the ground. The Lady says, "You are wondering, aren' t you, what all this may mean? Now, I will explain to you the reason for my coming today: 'Just as the snowflakes whirl over the earth and fall upon the ground in a thick layer, so the *prayer* and the *picture* will spread all over the world and penetrate into the hearts of all nations.'

"As the carpet of snow melts into the ground, so will the fruit, which is the Spirit come into the hearts of all those who say this prayer every day. For they are praying for the Holy Spirit to come down upon the earth. And now I speak to those who wish to see a miracle: 'Well now,' I tell them, 'Go and with great ardour and zeal set about this work of redemption and peace and you will see the miracle.' This is My message for today, for indeed *time presses*. A great movement has to be set on foot for the Son, for the Cross, and for the Advocate, the bearer of peace and tranquility – 'The Lady of All Nations.'

"You child, will have to co-operate without fear of dread. Spiritually and physically you will suffer. Later they will understand what My intention was. I shall give you directions how to spread the message. I have brought you here today, so that, in quiet and repose, you may be able to transmit My message well. (Given in German).

"Tell them that it is urgent. The world is becoming so degenerate, so materialistic, that it is high time to bring the *simple faith* again among the people. And this is all they need – the Cross with the Son of Man. You, grown-ups of this world, do teach your children to return to the Cross. I shall help them as 'The Lady of All Nations.'

"And to your loving care, my child, I entrust all mankind. Look at me and have confidence." Then the Lady looks at me for a long time and I see Her slowly disappear, while She says, "This time is Our time."

THIRTY-FIRST APPARITION – 15th APRIL, 1951

I see that great bright light again. It is as though the Lady came forward very slowly out of that light and now she stands clearly before me. The Lady says nothing as yet; She only looks and smiles at me.

Thus she remains for a while and then She says, "Child, watch carefully once more." The Lady is pointing to the girdle round Her waist, for this is what She wants me to look at. Then the Lady speaks again: "You have reported everything correctly. You are on the right path. Only, have another good look at this cloth."

And then it would seem that the Lady removes the girdle from Her waist to show me how She puts it on. – She wraps it round Herself once and then a second time. She tucks in the end of the two-layered cloth on Her side, leaving one small end hanging down.

"Mark well, what this means," says the Lady. "this represents the loin-cloth of the Son. For I stand as the Lady in front of the Cross of the Son. This picture will precede – and the Lady repeats 'will precede' – a dogma, a new dogma. Now I will explain it to you. So listen carefully."

"The Son came into the world as the Redeemer of men and the work of redemption was the Cross, with *all* its sufferings both of body and spirit."

Then the Lady moves away from the Cross and I again stand before that large Cross. Once again those dreadful pains seize hold of me, more violently than every before. They seem to last for a long time until the Lady comes and stands in front of the Cross as if in a haze. I see the Lady as it were, writhing and then She begins to weep. Indescribable sorrow is written over Her whole face and the tears run down Her cheeks.

Then suddenly the Lady says, "Child!" and now She seems to transmit that suffering to me. First of all a spiritual lassitude comes over me, which I feel very keenly; and then I experience the same pains as before, yet not so vehemently as the first time. Suddenly, I seem to collapse and I say to the Lady, "I can bear it no longer." It continues for another moment and then all is over.

Once again the Lady show herself clearly in front of the Cross and says, "Listen well and be sure to grasp what I am going to explain to you. But first I repeat: the Son came into the world as the Redeemer of mankind. The work of redemption was the Cross. He was sent by the Father. Now, however, the Father and the Son wants to send 'the Lady' throughout the whole *world*. In the past, too, She went before the Son and followed Him. For this reason, I am now standing on the world, on the globe. The Cross stands firmly fixed, *implanted* in it."

"Now the Lady comes to stand in front of it, as the Son's Mother, who with Him has accomplished this work of redemption.

This picture speaks clearly and now is the time to bring it into the world, for the world is once more in need of *the Cross*."

"The Lady, however, really stands here as the 'Co-Redemptrix' and 'Advocate.' About this, much controversy will arise. The Church, Rome, however, should not be afraid to take up the struggle. It can only make the Church stronger and more powerful. This is what I say to the theologians. Furthermore, I say to them: give this matter your serious attention. Once again I say, the Son always chooses the humble and lowly for His work. Child, I hope you have understood this properly and can silence all objections. Now I speak to you in particular: make sure My message is spread promptly."

I say to the Lady "How can I do this! I am so much afraid."

Then the Lady says, "You are afraid? But I am helping you! You will find that it will spread as of its own accord. You are on the right road. It shall and must happen that the people who accept this prayer will promise to say it everyday. You cannot estimate the great value this will have. You do not know what the future has in store." And now the Lady lets me see what looks like *snakes*, crawling about the world, *all over* the globe.

Then the Lady resumes, "Men have not yet realized in *how serious* a plight the world is. Because people grow superficial, they cannot realize *how* much harm is being done to the faith." For a long time the Lady stands looking fixedly into the distance. Then She says, "Child, things at present are just like they were before the Son came. Therefore, I cannot insist enough that mankind, that Rome, that *all* join in the fight for the Son's cause. I know well enough that efforts are being made in some places, but that is a *far cry from* what is required for saving the world. And the world has to be saved from degeneration, disaster and war. Send this prayer and picture to those countries where the faith has been destroyed.

"And now I have a message for your director: Tell him that he knows what to do and how to act. I will help him and you will do what I say. For I wish to be 'the Lady of All Nations,' who in these times wants to help the world.

"Nobody knows which way to turn? Now then, get back to your simple faith and the world will regain peace."

Now the Lady disappears very slowly and I hear Her repeat, "This time is Our time."

THIRTY-SECOND APPARITION – 29th APRIL, 1951

I see a bright light and the Lady is slowly emerging from it. Now I see Her clearly standing before me and She says, "I stand here as 'the Lady of All Nations' and have just now come in order to demonstrate that I wish to be 'the Lady of All Nations.' Listen carefully. You see Me standing upon the earth in front of the Cross of the Son. You have passed on My message completely. Only the loin-cloth was not mentioned before. The Son did wear it. Tell them that.

"I stand here as the Co-Redemptrix and Advocate. Everything should be concentrated on that. Repeat this after Me: The new dogma will be the 'dogma of the Co-Redemptrix.' Notice, I lay special emphasis on 'Co.' I have said that it will arouse much controversy. Once again I tell you that the Church, 'Rome,' will carry it through and silence all objections. The Church, 'Rome,' will incur opposition and overcome it. The Church, 'Rome,' will become stronger and mightier in proportion to the resistance she puts up in the struggle.

"My purpose and my commission to you is none other than to urge the Church, the theologians, to wage this battle. For the Father, the Son, and the Holy Spirit wills to send the Lady, chosen to bear the Redeemer, into *this* world, as Co-Redemptrix and Advocate. I have said, "This time is Our time," By this I mean the following: The world is caught up in degeneration and superficiality. It is at a loss. Therefore, the Father sends Me to be the Advocate, to implore the Holy Spirit to come. For the world is not saved by force, the world will be saved by the Spirit. It is only ideas that rule the world. Know your responsibility then, Church of Rome. Get your ideas across; bring Christ back into the world once more."

Now the Lady leaves the Cross and I once more get those terrible pains acutely. This keeps on for a while and then I see the Lady as in a haze standing in front of the Cross. Then even worse spiritual and bodily sufferings afflict me. I feel so exhausted that I sink down and cry, "I cannot bear it longer."

Meanwhile, I see the Lady collapse beneath the Cross. She throws both Her arms around the feet of Her Son and weeps bitterly. After this the Lady rises and I see a sword coming from the right, its point directed against the Lady's heart. Then I hear the Lady say, "That was the sword thrust that has been foretold."

Then all my pain and depression of spirit are gone and once more I see the Lady clearly, standing before the Cross.

She looks at me and says, "Child, pass on correctly that those who fight and labor for the cause, which the Son desires to succeed, should do so with great ardour and zeal." The Lady smiles and says, "I will help them. I have taught you that simple prayer to the Father and the Son. See that it is made known throughout the world, among all the Nations. They all have a *right to it.* I assure you that the world will change.

"But as for you, my child, you need simply pass on what I tell you. Your director should carry out My Will in all simplicity. You ask how this is to be accomplished? Well, simply by making it known. Nothing else is needed for the present. This picture has only a preparatory function. Again I say: preparatory. It will be used as a preparatory work for peace and redemption. Later on, they will use the picture for the Co-Redemptrix.

"In the sufferings, both spiritual and bodily, the Lady, the Mother has shared. She has always gone before. As soon as the Father had elected Her, She was the Co-Redemptrix with the Redeemer, who came into the world as the Man-God. Tell that to your theologians.

"I know well, the struggle will be hard and bitter (and then the Lady smiles to Herself and seems to gaze into the far distance), *but the outcome is already assured.*"

Then, coming still closer, the Lady resumes. "Now you see Me standing here clearly, very clearly. This is the way the picture should be made know throughout the world. My child, insist upon it that these things are carried out. They should not hesitate; they should act. The situation is far too serious. Nobody realizes, just *how* serious.

"I also wish to be made known to those people who are being kept away from the Son. Do save the people who are forced to turn away from Him. You are in duty bound to do so. The world is degenerating, so much so, that it was necessary for the Father and the Son to send Me into the world, among *all the peoples,* in order to be their Advocate and to save them. Tell your theologians this." And then I see the Lady leave and again I hear Her say, "This time is Our time."

THIRTY-THIRD APPARITION – 31st MAY, 1951

The Lady is here again and She says, " I am here and have come to tell you that I wish to be 'Mary, The Lady of All Nations.' Look closely. I am standing before the Cross of the Redeemer. My head, My hands and My feet are those of a human being, as those of the Son of Man. The rest belongs to the Spirit. My feet are firmly planted upon the globe, for it is the wish of the Father and the Son to send Me into the world in these times as the 'Co-Redemptrix, Mediatrix and Advocate.' This will constitute a new and last Marian dogma. This picture will go before it. This dogma will be much disputed; and yet it will prevail.

"I have repeated these things to you so that you may once more make them clear to your director and the theologians and be able to refute their objections. Pay attention now and explain what I am show-ing you. This is the *last direction* I am giving you with regard to the picture: you thought, my child, that you were seeing clouds around the globe. But now look closely at what I am going to show you."

And now I see the clouds changing into sheep. From left to right, all around the globe, from out of the depths and from all sides,

I can see flocks of sheep emerging. Here and there I see a black one. Lambs are reposing at the foot of the globe. The sheep keep coming, some grazing, but most of them with heads upturned, as if looking straight at the Lady with the Cross. Others again look up at Her while quietly lying on the ground.

Then the Lady speaks to me again, "My child, imprint this image deeply on your mind and transmit it correctly: The flocks of sheep represent the peoples of the world who will not find rest until they achieve content and fix their eyes on the Cross, the center of this world."

"Now look at my hands and relate what your see." Now I see in the palms of Her hands what appear to be wounds already healed and from these, rays of light stream out, three from each hand, and diffuse themselves upon the sheep.

Smiling, the Lady adds, "These three rays are Grace, Redemption, and Peace. Through the grace of My Lord and Master, and for the love of mankind, the Father sent His only-begotten Son as Redeemer for the world. Now they both wish to send the Holy Spirit, the Spirit of Truth, Who alone can bring Peace. Hence: 'Grace, Redemption and Peace.' The Father and the Son wish, as at this very time, to send Mary, 'the Lady of All Nations' as Co-Redemptrix, Mediatrix and Advocate. – Now I have given you a clear and lucid explanation of the picture. *There is nothing more to be said.*

"You, child are the instrument, merely the instrument to pass on these things. Make sure that the prayer, which briefly and yet so urgently asks for the sending of the True, Holy Spirit, is spread as quickly as possible. Tell your director and all who co-operate in this that I promise that all who pray before the picture and ask the help of Mary, 'the Lady of All Nations.' will be given grace for soul and body, in the measure that the Son wishes. You should not regard this as a matter for a limited circle only, for I am 'the Lady of *All* Nations.' This picture must go from country to country, from town to town. That is what is meant by redemption. Now I have a message for your director and all those who co-operate in this work: Be conscious of your duty and do not hesitate to carry out everything I have said. Again I say: I promise to help all who are in spiritual and bodily distress, if they carry out My will, the Will of the Father."

Then the Lady waits a while and looks in front of Her and She continues, "Theologians, you should have no difficulty if you consider that the Lord and Master had predestined the Lady for sacrifice. For the sword had already been directed at the heart of the Mother.

"My meaning is that I have always gone before the Son in spiritual and physical sufferings.

"And now I speak to the women of the world: women of this world, do you know what being a woman means? 'Sacrifice.' Abandon your self-seeking and vanity and try to lead to the Cross, the center of everything, your children and all those who are still wandering at pasture. You yourselves, participate in the Sacrifice.

"And now I speak to the men of this world: to them I say: 'From you, men, should come the strength and the will to lead the world to the *Sole Prince* of this world, the Lord Jesus Christ.'

"I have explained to you, child, how important this message is for the world, You should see to it, that with the help of your director and others, it will be made known to the world. This is My wish for today. I desire to be 'the Lady of *All* Nations.' Go to work, promptly and with modern means."

And now the Lady slowly leaves with the words, "This time is Our time."

THIRTY-FOURTH APPARITION – 2nd JULY, 1951

I see the Lady again standing in a bright light. She looks around Her with a smile and says, "I am satisfied. Have a care that the making known of the message continues. I have spoken of the great movement for God that is to begin here; all should participate in it. Now watch well and listen. The following is the explanation of the new dogma: "As Co-Redemptrix, Mediatrix and Advocate I am standing on the globe in front of the Cross of the Redeemer. By the will of the Father, the Redeemer came on earth.

"To accomplish this, the Father used the Lady. Thus, from the Lady the Redeemer received only – I am stressing the word 'only' – flesh and blood, that is to say, the body. From My Lord and Master the Redeemer received His divinity.

"In this way, the Lady became Co-Redemptrix. I have told you: 'This time in Our time.' This means that the Father and the Son wants in these times to send the Co-Redemptrix, Mediatrix and Advocate throughout the whole world."

For a long time the Lady remains standing before me in silence. Then, looking at Her hands, She resumes, "Now look hard at My hands. From them emanate rays of Grace, Redemption and Peace. The rays shine upon all peoples, upon all sheep. Among these peoples there are many of good will. To be of good will means to keep the first and great commandment. The *first* and *great* commandment is LOVE. He who loves, will honour his Lord and Creator in His Creation. He who loves, will do nothing that would dishonour his neighbour. That is what this world is lacking: Love of God – *Love of Neighbour.*

"'This time is Our time.' All peoples must honour the Lord and Master in His Creation. All peoples should pray for the True and Holy Spirit. Therefore, I have given you this short and powerful prayer.

"Thus I repeat once again: The prayer must speedily be spread abroad. The whole world is degenerating. Let the men of good will pray every day that the True Spirit may come! I am 'the Lady of All Nations.' 'This time is Our time.' Mary just as *Mary.* Now, however, in this new era, which is beginning now, I wish to be 'the Lady of All Nations.' *Everybody* will understand this.

"Tell your director. Say that I am satisfied with everything, and I am stressing the word '*everything.*' As to you, my child, *I urge you to carry out My will and to make it known.* Have no fear. Make it known!"

The Lady slowly disappears.

THIRTY-FIFTH APPARITION – 15th AUGUST, 1951

I see the Lady. She says, "Today, I have come as 'the Lady of All Nations.'" Then the Lady motions around Her and, looking at me, says, "I have crushed the snake with My foot. I have become united to My Son as I had always been united with Him. This is 'the dogma' that has gone before in the history of the Church. As Co-Redemptrix, Mediatrix and Advocate I stand here, now in this time, in Our time. The dogma of the Assumption had to precede it. The last and greatest dogma will follow. The Sacrifice stands and will stand at the center of the world, *in this era."*

Now the Lady moves away from the Cross and once again I get violent pains. Afterwards, She resumes Her position before the Cross and I am greatly distressed at the sight of Her suffering. And now I see a bright light radiating from the Cross.

The Lady says, "Mankind has been entrusted to the Mother.

"For the Son said, 'Woman behold thy son; son behold thy Mother' – this, Co-Redemptrix, Mediatrix and Advocate. Inform your theologians. Tell them that I wish to be and shall be, the Co-Redemptrix, Mediatrix and Advocate.

"This picture will go before; this picture shall be spread. Tell your director: I am satisfied with everything, including the prudence, but...'the Lady of All Nations' will assert Her place in the world. This is the will of the Father and the Son, with whom I have been wholly re-united. Just as the Son had known Me (on earth), so He took Me back again. The last Marian dogma – the Lady standing in front of the Cross as the Co-Redemptrix in this present time – will be the principal one."

"I have said, *disasters will come, catastrophes of nature;* I have said, the great ones will disagree among themselves. I have said the world is on the way to ruin, wherefore the Father and the Son *now* sends the Lady, such as She was, back to the world. The Lady was once known as 'Mary.' The world is on its way to ruin, is ruined already. Holland is on the brink of total degeneration, there I have to put My foot on Holland. From Holland I want to give a message to the whole world. My other foot is placed on Germany. The Mother of God weeps for the children of Germany (*'Die Muttergottes weint uber die Kinder Deutschlands'*). They have always been My children and, therefore, from Germany also I wish to be made know to the world as 'the Lady of All Nations.'"

"I shall help you and all who share in the responsibility. I even want all this to penetrate into those countries that are cut off from the others. There too 'the Lady of All Nations' will bestow Her blessing. *See to it;* do not hesitate. I never hesitated myself. I anticipated my Son's Calvary. This picture shall go before. This picture shall be spread throughout the world.

Rome, do you know, how completely everything is being undermined? The years will speed by unheeded, but the longer you wait, the more the Faith will decline; the greater the number of years, the greater the apostasy."

"The Lady of All Nations stands here and says, 'I wish to help them and I am permitted to help them.' The first and great commandment is Love. He who possesses love, will honour his Lord and Master in His Creation, that is to say, recognize the sublime in His Creation, inclusive of the Sacrifice.

"He who possesses love, will do to others everything, he would like to be done to himself. Love is the first and great commandment that Christ has given. This is what I wish to announce today. This message *must* be passed on. You are the instrument. The Church will be attacked greatly over the new dogma. It will arouse astonishment in others. The Church, however, will thereby gain in power and strength.

"Do you know how great your power is, Rome? Do you realize what your task in hand is? Quite simply to lead men to the good life, to Christ. Other little things are unimportant. I wish to be 'the Lady of All Nations.' I will and can obtain grace, redemption and peace for all who ask. I promise that today.

"You, My child, must be content to wait. Your director should not be so much afraid. Make all nations of one mind. Let all people be one in Jesus Christ."

And now the Lady slowly disappears.

THIRTY-SIX APPARITION – 20th SEPTEMBER, 1951

There is the Lady again. She looks at me for a long time without a word. Then the Lady begins to speak and says, "I am called 'Miriam' or 'Mary.' *Now* I wish to be 'the Lady of All Nations.' My child, let them know that the time presses." Now I see a large 52 before me. The Lady continues, "Great and important events are drawing near – in the spiritual, economic and material spheres. In the spiritual realm – spiritual undermining!

"Christians all over the world should unite. Are the Christians really conscious of what the others are doing and of the sacrifices they make for their ideals? The Church must be ready to meet great dangers. Christians shall and must enter into themselves. Let them consider what part they are to play in this world! Once again I warn Rome and I tell the Holy Father, 'You are the fighter' of this time; see to it that all your subjects prove to be great-hearted and open-minded in their work and in their judgments. Alone in this way can the world be won for the Faith."

Now all at once I see snowflakes whirling around the Lady and these fall upon the globe. The Lady then says, "Child, why is this prayer not being spread abroad? What are they waiting for? I have taught it to you, so that it might be circulated among the people. Let everyone say this short and simple prayer every day! This prayer is purposely kept short and simple, so that every person may manage to say it, even in this modern and speed-mad world. It has been given, so that the coming of the *Spirit of Truth* may be implored for the world." Now the Lady looks about Her and then at the world., Then I see black patches appear here and there. The Lady says to me, "These are the economic and material disasters that will strike the world. I have said: *disasters will come, disasters of nature.* Now I say to you: all these black patches you see there, are disasters yet to come. And now I do not only speak of catastrophes of nature.Once again I call on all the Christian peoples when I say, '*It is high time! Band yourselves together.*' And you, child, will hand it on. You will let the world know that is the 'Lady of All Nations' who is sending you. You will tell the theologians to see their battle for the Marian dogma through to the finish. I shall help them. 'The Lady of All Nations' will reach out to the whole earth.

"To the countries that have rejected me, I shall return as 'the Lady of All Nations,' standing on the globe in front of the Cross, with the flock of Christ around Me. This is how I wish to and will come.

"I shall listen to the requests of those who call upon me under the title of 'the Lady of All Nations,' as the Son desires it. The Lord and Master will be served and honored in His Creation. Men shall obey the First and Great Commandment among themselves. I wish to be called, 'the Lady of All Nations' in these times.

"Because the present world is pining for solidarity in everything that concerns itself, the Lord and Master wants to give the people of this world *Spiritual Oneness.* For this reason, He sends

'Mariam' or 'Mary' as the 'Lady of All Nations.' The Religious Orders should play a large part in propagating the Message. The Holy Father should give his blessing to this work. For he is the 'fighter' of this period. He will be taken up to dwell with Us." And now I see the Pope standing next 'the Lady of All Nations' in an indescribable light and She places a crown on his head and a Cross in his right hand. Then all this vanishes from my sight and the Lady again stands in front of me by herself. She says, "Child, you will pass on everything properly and tell your director. So be it!"

Then the Lady slowly disappears.

THIRTY-SEVENTH APPARITION
15th NOVEMBER, 1951

I see the Lady standing there. She says, "Tell the world that I wish to be the 'Lady of All Nations.' Let the world pray to the Lord Jesus Christ, Son of the Father, that He send the Holy Spirit, so that the Spirit of Truth may dwell in the hearts of all nations. Ask that the Lady of All Nations, who once was Mary, may be the Advocate. 'The Lady of All Nations' is standing here, before the Cross of Her Son. Her feet are placed on the center of the earth; around Her is the flock of Jesus Christ. I come as the Co-Redemptrix-Mediatrix at this time. Co-Redemptrix I was already *at the Annunciation.*

(Now I ask the Lady what this means). "This means that the *Mother* became Co-Redemptrix by the *Will* of the Father. Tell your theologians this. Tell them, moreover, that this will be the last dogma in Marian history.

"This picture shall prepare the way. Have this picture brought to the world; and thereby I mean the whole world, not only your country. The world is degenerating. The world is being afflicted with *disaster upon disaster.* The world will be and is – *economically and materially* at a dead end. Wars will continue until the *Spirit of Truth* comes with His help. Get the people back to the Cross."

Then the Lady points at the globe. I am overcome with great terror as I see the globe turning black. On closer examination, I find that it is not equally black everywhere, but very dark in the East. Then the Lady says, "Child, do pass this on well: the peoples of the world should keep ONE Commandment before their eyes and that is LOVE. He who possesses *Love,* will serve the Lord and Master in His Creation. Keep in mind this one commandment – *Love.* If that is brought back among the people, the world will be saved." Then the Lady, again lifting Her finger in warning, says, "Christian people, *the heathens of this world want to be your teachers."*

Then She continues, "Christians, know your duty! Now I am addressing the Church of Rome and I say to the Pope, 'See that all your subjects know how to bring back the Charity of Jesus Christ to this world – this *degenerate world!* The Church of Rome must fulfill this precept to the utmost of its power. And then I say, *be broadminded.* Try to establish yourself in this *modern* world with Jesus Christ on the Cross. Study to understand these words fully and carry them into effect. This world can be saved only through the Church that holds this doctrine.'

"I am now speaking to England when I say, '*I shall come back.* You, England, will be hit in your dominions. You, England, will not be able to continue without the help of others. Catholics of England, realize your duty and work for the Church of Rome. Bring 'the Lady of All Nations' to England.' America, 'Where do you stand? Dare you carry through...? It is 'the Lady of All Nations' who asks you this.' (This the Lady said angrily).

"Look," says the Lady, "where I have placed one foot – this one is on Germany and the other on Holland. And then I say: 'Poor German people, haven' t you learned your lesson yet? Do not be deceived by honeyed words. Christians of Germany, *return to the Cross* and ask 'the Lady of All Nations' that She may help Germany. This must become a great movement.'

"Now I speak to your own country and I say, 'Holland, look out! Your people too, Holland, have taken the wrong turning.'"

Now I see that the Lady points to France as She says, "France, you will be and have been destroyed in your faith." Then I see France all red. The Lady resumes, "France, – and now I am addressing the great ones- you will save your country only by taking it back to the Cross and 'Votre Dame.' Your people must be guided back to 'the Lady of All Nations.'"

"Italy, you have had your crosses. Remain on your guard. Rome, remember your poor people. And now once again I speak to the Pope and say, 'You are *the fighter.'* You are 'the preserver' of this world. You will be taken up to dwell among Us. This Pope will be revered by all the nations of the world.

"Now I am speaking to the whole world when I say: 'Nations, whoever or whatever you may be, turn to your Creator, with all you needs. Oh, learn to find HIM, wherever you are. Ask 'the Lady of All Nations' that She be your Advocate.'"

Now the Lady, looking at me with a smile, says, "Child, tell them I am pleased with the beginnings of the movement. Tell all those you co-operate with, to spread the prayer-picture in even *greater numbers* and farther afield. I shall assist them.

"And now I am speaking to you in particular, child: you should always come before this picture, and I say: *'this'* picture, in order to pray for all people in bodily or spiritual need. You should continue to do so, until the end has come. I have My special intention concerning this picture; you will hear of this later. Tell your director: so be it."

Then I see the Lady slowly disappearing.

THIRTY-EIGHTH APPARITION – 31st DECEMBER, 1951

The Lady is here again. For a long time She looks at me with a smile. Then She begins to speak and say, "My child, look and listen carefully to what I have come to tell you today. I am not bringing a *new doctrine*. The teaching is correct, but the laws can be changed."

Now the Lady points to the globe and suddenly I see Rome lying before me. Then the Lady says, "Tell the Pope that he is on the right road. You must let him know this because people *think otherwise*. The Spirit of Justice and Truth must always reign over the world. Once more I say: this Pope is on the right road. And yet again I say, 'This time is Our time.'

"And now I shall explain to you the reason for my coming again: I do not come to bring a new doctrine. The doctrine is already there. I have come to give you another message. Make sure you pass it on correctly."

Now again the Lady allows me to see Her picture clearly. It looks as though She came forward. Then the Lady says, "Transmit the following exactly: the Father, The Lord and Master, has willed the Handmaid of the Lord to come into this world as 'Miriam.' or 'Mary.' She was chosen from among *all women* as Co-Redemptrix, Mediatrix and Advocate. Say to your theologians: She was made Co-Redemptrix *already at the beginning.*

"'This time is Our time.' Now the Father and the Son want to be asked to send the Spirit. I have taught you that simple prayer and let you see how I wish to have it spread over the world. Well then, carry these direction into effect. The simple prayer has been given for the benefit of all nations. Do your work and see to it that it is made know everywhere."

Then, I say to the Lady, "How can I do this, if I am being prevented all the time?"

The Lady smiles at me, saying, "You should do what I say. Go to your Bishop and tell him that I desire to be 'the Lady of All Nations,' who is sent by the Father at this time. Once more I wish to make it clear: The Church of Rome should refrain from everything that is in conflict with its teaching. All right then, this movement is not in conflict with its teaching. Time presses: consider that well. All nations groan under the yoke of Satan. How much he is gaining ground, nobody can tell. I warn all people of the world. Time is serious and pressing. Now a favourable moment has come for the Church of Rome. She will become stronger in the measure the fight increases.

"'The Lady of All Nations' stands in the middle of the world in front of the Cross. She enters times as 'Co-Redemptrix, Mediatrix and Advocate.' She will pass into Marian history *under this title.* The *new* and *last* dogma in Marian History will be the dogma of the 'Co-Redemptrix and Mediatrix.' Now I stand as Advocate in these anxious times. All of you, *whoever or whatever* you may be, ask that the Holy Spirit of Truth may descend. You shall beg this of the Father and Son. The Blessed Trinity will reign over the world again. The Lady stands here as the Advocate. It is the Creator we are concerned with and not the Lady. Tell you theologians. Ask them to send this prayer over the world and the Lady will give them the ability and the strength to carry it through."

Now the Lady points to the globe, saying, "I will let you see what is going to happen. It is by dint of terrible *strife and calamity* that the world with all those who have turned away from the Blessed Trinity, will come back to the Church. Therefore, I repeat again: Rome, seize your opportunity. Be large-hearted and let *Love* rule your actions. Love can save this chaotic world.

"Bring all nations back to their Creator. Teach them all how simple it is to see the *Creator*. Men should treat their neighbours as themselves. A simpler doctrine does not exist. Let each one hold fast to these two things and you have the Church of Rome securely in your hands. Simple faith is what can save mankind.

"In Russia a great change will come about." Then the Lady pauses before She says, very slowly and distinctly, "After much conflict.

"China will turn to the Mother Church." – Again the Lady pauses before adding very slowly, "After much conflict."

"America, remember your *Faith*. Do not sow wrong ideas and confusion among your people and abroad. 'The Lady of All Nations' exhorts America to remain what it has been.

"Europe, you should seek to establish *peace* among yourselves. Help those who are in need – in spiritual need. Get ready for the combat – the spiritual combat. 'The Lady of All Nations' wishes to reach *all people, no matter who or what they may be*. This is why She has received this title from Her Lord and Master.

"You, my child, should not be afraid to pass on this message. I shall help you and all those who join in the work. Tell your director on behalf of 'the Lady of All Nations' that he should take part in the work of spreading this message. Tell him not to be afraid and to do what is being said. He should ask permission for it – simply getting the prayer-picture sent out into the world.

"'The Lady of All Nations' promises here and now that those who ask will be heard, if it is the Will of the Father, the Son and the Holy Spirit. The prayer has been given for the salvation of the world. This prayer has been given for the conversion of the world. Let this prayer accompany whatever you do in your daily life. *This prayer should be spread in the churches and through modern means of communication.*

"The people of the present world should learn to invoke 'the Lady of All Nations' – who once was 'Mary' – as their advocate, so that the world may be delivered from degeneration, disaster and war. Tell your theologian this! 'This time in Our time, Come and pray before this picture.'" And now the Lady slowly disappears.

THIRTY-NINTH APPARITION – 17th FEBRUARY, 1952

The Lady is standing here again. She moves very close up to me saying, "Listen carefully and tell your theologians and all the nations that they should try to understand My message and explain it well.

"The Lord Jesus Christ came and brought with Him the Church and the Cross as a gift from the Lord and Creator. The Church is and will remain. The Lord and Creator brought the Church into the world through the Son. The Lord and Creator demands gratitude from the creature.

"The Church is the Community of Nations whose business it is to adore and worship their Lord and Creator – the Father, the Son and the Holy Spirit.

"All those who are in charge of the Community, should see to it that the Church will continue and expand. 'This time is Our time.' The Lord and Creator deems it necessary to send the Church a warning through 'the Lady of All Nations.' The time has come. Inform the theologians. The Church, Rome, is now getting its chance.

"All the Christians of the present time are responsible for the successive generations. Tell the Pope it is all right. Through the Will of the Lord and Master 'the Lady of All Nations' will assist him. The Pope should carry everything out. This Pope is 'the fighter' and the Holy Father of the Christians at the present time and of the future.

"The nations hereafter will venerate him. He will be taken up to dwell with Us. The Church is and remains. The doctrine is and stands.

"Their expression and the laws, however, can be changed with the help of the Holy Spirit. Tell your theologians this! Christ, the Son of the Father, brought with Him the Cross to the world. With the Cross came the Sacrifice."

Now the Lady waits in silence for a long time. Then She resumes, "The Lord and Master selected a Woman, called 'Miriam' or 'Mary,' from among all the peoples of the world. She was destined, through the Will of the Father, to bring the Son of Man into the world, together with His Church and the Cross. The Lady was the Handmaid of the Lord. She bore the Son of Man through the Will of the Father and was thus necessarily allied with the Church and the Cross. This Woman stands in front of you in this present time as the Co-Redemptrix, Mediatrix and Advocate. Let the following works sink in well: the (Woman or) 'Lady of All Nations' *can* and *will* bestow on all the peoples of the world, who have recourse to Her – grace, redemption and peace. To you all, however, falls the task of introducing 'the Lady of All Nations' to the whole world."

Now the Lady draws my attention to the globe. I see the globe rotating under Her feet and everywhere snow is falling thickly. "Do you see?" resumes the Lady "Just like this 'the Lady of All Nations' shall be brought all over the world, from country to country, from town to town. Let them become One Community! – Through that simple prayer this will be realized. Ask your Bishop if he would kindly sanction the complete version of the prayer: 'May the Lady of All Nations, who once was Mary, be our Advocate!' Inform your Bishop that 'the Lady of All Nations' will help and assist him; and that the work of spreading really *must* go ahead.

"Say that the time has not yet come. 'The Lady of All Nations' has to be sent out first. The sign of 'the Lady of all Nations' will later be seen over the whole world. Let them understand this well! Sham powers will fall."

Here the Lady waits a long time and then resumes, "Rome, the Church, should occupy herself with the peoples of this present world. The sheep must be gathered into *one* fold. You, Christians, each one of you individually, take the Cross in your hands. With the crucifix in your hand, you shall posses the kingdom. With the crucifix in your hand, you shall meet your neighbour. With the crucifix in your hand, you shall vanquish your foe. Only thus will the Christians of this world feel themselves one with the Church and with the Cross. The nations must be made more and more familiar with the 'Memorial' of the Lord Jesus Christ.

Bishops, you can take care of that. You can see to it that the Sacrifice becomes an increasingly communal celebration. Understand these words well."

The Lady pauses a while. Then She adds, "The Christians have thus been given a warning. Take your place, all of you, at the foot of the Cross and draw strength from the Sacrifice; and the pagans will not overwhelm you. I ask the bishops and priests alike to come to the aid of this world, these children of men. I will stand by them. The Lord Jesus Christ , Son of the Father, will give the Holy Spirit of Truth, if all of you pray for it. I repeat: 'The Lady of All Nations' can and will bring the promised grace, redemption and peace.

"And now, child, I am speaking to you: charge yourself with the spread of the devotion. Let that be your *whole concern*; and help both spiritually and physically by saying the prayer of 'the Lady of All Nations.' Come before this picture and pray. When the time has come, I shall give you a message concerning this painting. Let them know this. Say that the picture is meant for everyone."

Now the Lady slowly disappears.

FORTIETH APPARITION – 19th MARCH, 1952

I was sitting before the painting, praying for the Holy Father. Suddenly a voice begins to speak and I see 'the Lady of All Nations' standing before me. She says, "Tell the Holy Father that 'the Lady of All Nations' will give him his sign. The Church, Rome, will have to face a terrible struggle. Before the year 2000 much will have changed in the Church, the Community. Nevertheless, the substance will remain." Now I see sheep running as it were helter-skelter round the globe and many taking flight. The Lady points at it and says, "Do you see that? The Church – the sheep – have been dispersed and still more will take to flight. 'The Lady of All Nations,' however, will bring them back into one fold." And again the Lady says, "Into one fold."

"Ask your Bishop to pray to 'the Lady of All Nations' and I shall give him a sign. You should all pray to 'the Lady of All Nations.' And you, child, come before this painting and pray as long as you can."

Then, all of a sudden, the Lady has gone.

FORTY-FIRST APPARITION – 6th April, 1952

The Lady is here again! She says, "Now you must listen and transmit carefully what I have come to say today. Tell the theologians that I am not pleased about their alteration of the prayer, 'May the Lady of All Nations, who once was Mary, be our Advocate' – that must remain as it is. 'This time is Our time.' Pass on the following to the theologians: 'The Lady' came with the Sacrifice of the Cross: The Son said to His Mother, 'Woman behold thy son.' So you see, it was at the Sacrifice of the Cross that the change came about.

"The Lord and Master chose 'Mirian' or 'Mary' from among all the women, to become the 'Mother' of His Divine Son. At the Sacrifice of the Cross, however, she became the 'Lady' ('Woman') – the Co-Redemptrix and Mediatrix. – This was announced by the Son at the time that He returned to His Father.

"Therefore, I bring this new wording into these times, and say, 'I am the Lady of All Nations, who once was Mary.' Let the theologians know. These words have that significance for the theologians.

"'This time in Our time.' The forthcoming dogma is the last Marian dogma, namely 'the Lady of All Nations' as the 'Co-Redemptrix, Mediatrix and Advocate.' At the Sacrifice of the Cross the Son announced this title to the whole world. Whoever or whatever you are, I am for you 'The Lady.'

"I have come to tell this unhinged and degenerate world; join forces, all of you. You, Christians, will find one another at the feet of 'the Lady of All Nations,' just as you find one another beneath the Cross of the Son.

"Much will have to be changed in the Community, which is the Church. You, people, whoever or whatever you may be, support and help one another. In the first and chief Commandment you will find everything you are in need of. 'May the Lady of All Nations, who once was Mary, be our Advocate!'

"The Lady wishes especially to come to those places where She used to be and where She has never yet been.

"Yours is a great task," says the Lady to me. "Let all those who co-operate in this great work, do so in all earnestness and with great zeal. Your task, my child, has not come to an end yet. Tell your Bishop to pass on the prayer to the whole world. I shall help him. I shall likewise assist your director, till the end.

"Say to the Pope that all is *well*. He will know what I mean. Tell the Pope to get everything ready for the new dogma. Tell him also that he should prepare all the changes and discuss them with those who have been appointed by him. Tell him that now the time is at hand. 'The Lady of All Nations' will watch over the Community. Let all ask 'the Lady of All Nations' through this simple prayer, and the Lady shall help them in the measure willed by the Father and the Son. She was Mary, 'the Handmaid of the Lord.' She now desires to be 'the Lady of All Nations.' Whoever or whatever you are, come to 'the Lady of All Nations.' I warn all the Christians and say: do realize the gravity of the times. Join your hands in prayer. Go and plant the Cross in the midst of the world. You are all responsible for the task that falls to you in this present time. Resist the influence of the wrong spirit. Pray every day that the Lord Jesus Christ, Son of the Father, may send the Holy Spirit over the earth, and 'the Lady of All Nations,' who once was 'Mary,' will be your Advocate. So be it!"

And then the Lady is gone.

FORTY-SECOND APPARITION – 15th JUNE, 1952

"Once more I am here, 'the Lady of All Nations.'" Now the Lady looks at me for a long time without speaking, then says, "In the foregoing message, I explained to you the significance of the title of 'the Lady of All Nations.' Today I have come to tell you that the great movement for 'the Lady of All Nations' must begin *now*. Deliver the message to the world. 'The Lady of All Nations' will help you and all those who will fight for this. The great movement must begin! This picture has to prepare the way. Later on, there will be no nation without 'the Lady of All Nations.' This title begins to operate *now*. 'This time is Our time.'"

After this the Lady gazes in front of Her for a long time. Then She begins to speak again, saying, – "'The Lady, who once was Mary.' Only at the departure of the Lord Jesus Christ did co-redemption have its beginning. Only when the Lord Jesus Christ went away, did She become the Mediatrix and Advocate. When departing, the Lord Jesus Christ gave to the nations 'The Lady of All Nations.' Now the time has come for Her to announce this title to the world. Tell your theologians this. Tell your Bishop that I am satisfied. The right version of the prayer is now being spread. Tell all those who participate that they must say this prayer.

"Let the regular and secular clergy work together! Not only in this, but in other matters as they will have to co-operate more readily with one another. Are you not the apostles of the Master? Seek and find one another. If the apostles are not one in their outlook, how can the nations be *one?*

"I implore the Church of Rome again and again: be of one mind and heart in maintaining the one Truth, the Lord and Creator of this world – the Father, the Son and the Holy Spirit. This present time is the time of the Holy Spirit. All of you must ask the Holy Spirit to make His Truth prevail over the world.

"Moral decline prevails in the world at the moment. People in higher positions only strive after power; people in higher positions think only of material things. People are being bewildered and led in the wrong direction."

Then the Lady points at the globe and says, "Just look at all those countries! Nowhere is unity to be found, nowhere peace, nowhere repose for the nations. Everywhere there is tension, everywhere anxiety. The Lord Jesus Christ lets this be. *His* time will come. There will be an intervening period of unrest – caused by *humanism, paganism, godlessness, snakes.* These will attempt to control the world.

"Today I have come to say that the great campaign against all this must now begin. And now I speak to your theologians and say: do in all sincerity acknowledge the importance of this matter.

"And to those I first chose for this cause I say: you must help with all the means in your power to take the spreading of the message in hand, each one in his own way. Now the time is at hand, the time of 'the Lady of All Nations.' I shall help them."

Now the Lady stands in silence and looks at me intently. She says, "To you, child, I still say this, 'You have a great task to accomplish. Take courage and fear not. 'The Lady of All Nations' is standing before you. This painting is to stay here (in Germany) for the present. The Lady will give the sign.'"

Then the Lady slowly leaves.

FORTY-THIRD APPARITION – 5th OCTOBER, 1952

"I am here again. I have come to deliver a special message. Pass on everything well.

"Never has 'Mirian or Mary' in the Community, the Church been *officially* called 'Co-Redemptrix. Never has She *officially* been called 'Mediatrix.' Never has She *officially* been called 'Advocate.' These three thoughts are not only closely connected, they form one whole. Therefore, this will be the keystone of Marian history; it will become the dogma of the Co-Redemptrix, Mediatrix and Advocate.

"I do not reproach the theologians if I say: why can you not come to an agreement about this dogma? Once more I shall explain it and make it clearer still: The Father sent the Lord Jesus Christ as the 'Redeemer of All Nations.' The Lord Jesus Christ was this from the beginning. He became this in the Sacrifice and in His going to the Father.

"'Miriam or Mary' became the Handmaid of the Lord, chosen by the Father and the Holy Spirit. From the beginning She was in virtue of this choice, the Co-Redemptrix, Mediatrix and Advocate of All Nations. Only at the departure of the God-Man, the Lord Jesus Christ, She became the Co-Redemptrix, Mediatrix and Advocate. When leaving, in one final act, the Lord Jesus Christ gave Miriam or Mary to the nations, gave *Her* as 'the Lady of All Nations.'

"He spoke the words: 'Woman, behold thy son; son, behold thy Mother – ONE act! – and by this, Miriam or Mary received this new title.'

"How is it that this new title – 'the Lady of all Nations' – only now enters the world? It is because the Lord reserved it for this present time. The other dogmas had to come first; just as Her life on earth had to precede 'the Lady of All Nations.' All previous dogmas comprised the mortal life and the leaving of this life by the Lady. For the theologians, this simple explanation should suffice. It was necessary to give this explanation once more."

"Now I ask you, child, to listen carefully again: tell all who are placed over you and those who are helping you, *that now the time is at hand.* Fear nothing; you will eventually get to your Holy Father. Fear nothing: 'the Lady of All Nations' will give him a sign.

Then you must tell the Holy Father that he is 'the fighter' and the pioneer of this new era. Assure him of the support of the Lord and the Lady in his difficult and arduous task. He should prepare everything and set it on its way (he knows what I am referring to) for the coming times. 'This time is Our time.' A heavy burden rests upon his shoulder. Let him make sure that everything he says and wishes is carried into effect by the Community – the Church. Tell him that. You will get there, my child, and you must not hesitate or be afraid to tell him *everything,* that 'the Lady of All Nations' has come to tell you. For it is She who gave you these messages. All She requires of you is to be the instrument and to obey Her."

(Now I tell "the Lady" within myself that I have nothing to offer and that I do not understand why She chooses me for this. The Lady answers,) "You are telling Me that you have nothing to offer by empty hands. The Lady simply asks you to pass these messages on to those who have need of them. *The Lady does the rest.* Be faithful. Help the people who are in need – and it is spiritual need I am referring to. You can help by saying the prayer. More is not asked. Tell your director to be at peace, that everything is all right. The Lady will help him also.

"Now I am speaking to all priests and religious: you are all apostles and handmaids of the Father, the Son and the Holy Spirit. The Lady is not now going to blame you. She knows She is dealing with human beings. Life is difficult for you these days; but still I exhort you to act in the Spirit of your Lord and Master Jesus Christ. He has gone before you, as God, as Man. Be apostles among each other. Are you not all one? Each one must be an apostle on his own account. Be of one mind among yourselves. How can the Church – the Community – be great and united if you are divided among yourselves? Heed my warning and try to be sincere and kind to one another. No, the Lady does not reproach you, but, like a loving Mother, comes to warn the apostles of the Church against false prophets, against the wrong spirit.

"You must all say the prayer I have given you. 'The Lady of All Nations' has been sent especially at the present time in order to overcome the spiritual decline and degeneration. All of you who are in spiritual need, have recourse to 'the Lady of All Nations,' and She will help you.

"Next, I say to the apostles of this time: be broadminded, be merciful. Be honest with the people. Evaluate and judge in the same way as the Lord Jesus Christ did. Try to read the signs of the times you live in and realize what the struggle is about. Realize that it is for men's minds. This is the time of the Spirit. The fight is hard and bitter, but the True Spirit will triumph, provided that all of you join in the cause. Church of Rome, seize your opportunity.

"The Father, the Son and the Holy Spirit now wants to make His Church great. Make sure you understand your doctrine. It was necessary for the Lady to come and say all this. Remember the First and Great Commandment – *Love.* That embraces everything.

"Finally I speak to (name of donor of picture) – I am satisfied with you. Three sacrifices the Lord had demanded of you. Now the Lady is asking you for something. You have offered this painting to the Lady as a gift. This picture is however destined for all peoples: for everyone who wishes to come to 'the Lady of All Nations.' Go and present your picture to them. It is the wish of the Lady that it should go to the Netherlands and in particular, to Amsterdam. The Lady has Her special reason for this. Amsterdam is the city of the miraculous Host. There 'the Lady of All Nations' also will go."

Holland is on the way to ruin. The Lady still wants to preserve this country from this calamity and has, therefore, set Her foot upon it. She has willed the movement to originate here (in Germany); the painting, however, She desires to have in Amsterdam. Make this sacrifice, hand it over to the Dominicans. Note well: the offerings that will be made are not for the Dominicans alone, but for everything in connection with the *church.* 'The Lady of All Nations' wishes to entrust the painting to the care of the Dominicans. Though that is no special prerogative, as it is destined for all people. Later, I shall come here to speak about this in particular." And slowly now the Lady leaves.

FORTY-FOURTH APPARITION – 8th DECEMBER, 1952

"My message of today is destined for all nations: I am entering these times as 'Co-Redemptrix, Mediatrix and Advocate.' In one act the Lord gave Mary these three titles – gave these three concepts in one significant act. The new dogma will be much disputed; therefore, I have given you that detailed explanation.

The time is at hand. Tell the Pope's Sacristan to inform the Pope. He must bring 'the Lady of All Nations' to him. The Pope should prepare this dogma and offer it for consideration. Tell him the time is ripe. The Holy Spirit must come upon this world. Let the Holy Father not be hesitant about his decisions. For he is 'the fighter.' I shall give him My sign. I have said this picture is to prepare the way. This picture must be spread all over the world. It is the illustration of the new dogma. This is why I have personally given this picture to the nations. The prayer will remain to the end. The prayer that Mary as 'the Lady of All Nations' has presented to the world, will have to be said in all churches. You should employ your modern means to achieve this. Ask permission and it will be granted to you. Know well: the time is drawing near."

After a moments pause, the Lady says very slowly and distinctly, "53."

She indicates the globe on which She stands and says, "We are on the eve of weighty decisions. We are on the eve of great oppression. The enemy of our Lord Jesus Christ has worked slowly but effectively. His posts are manned. His work is almost finished. Nations, take warning: the spirit of untruth, lies and deceit, is carrying many away. The decisive day is beginning."

The Lady silently gazes in front of Her. Then She resumes. *"Great threatening dangers hang over the world. The Churches will be undermined still more."*

After another thoughtful silence, the Lady adds, "You must realize why I come as 'the Lady of All Nations.' I come in order to rally all nations in the Spirit, in the Spirit of Truth. All men must learn to find the Holy Spirit. Strive after justice, truth and love. Do not reject your brothers. Lead them on to the knowledge of the True Spirit. A heavy responsibility rests upon the people of these times.

"Educators and parents, take care of the young. Do show them the way to the *True* Church – the Community. – It was necessary for the Lord to send Mary, His Handmaid, into these times as 'the Lady of All Nations.' I warn the world and therefore I bring this message.

"Now once more I speak to all apostles and all religious." (Now the Lady looks very concerned). Then the Lady says, "Listen well to a loving Mother. She wants to help you, too, in these times. Say this prayer and implore the intercession of 'the Lady of All Nations' and She will help you. Be just, sincere and charitable to one another. Co-operate in the *one* great cause of making the Church reach out to everyone. Let the regular and secular clergy understand one another and work together for the one great cause! Are you not all the same?"

In thoughtful silence the Lady again looks in front of Her. After a long time She says, slowly and clearly, "Know how to evaluate and judge after the example of the Lord Jesus Christ. 'The Lady of All Nations' cannot impress this upon you enough. Listen to My words, which in these anxious times I am allowed to speak.

"I am speaking to all when I say, 'You have no idea how serious and *how difficult* these times are.'"

Another pause, while the Lady gazes into the distance. "The Pope of Rome," the Lady resumes, "has a heavier task than any of his predecessors. People, do help the Holy Father. Imitate his example. Follow the precepts of the Encyclicals. Let the world be filled with their teaching! For then the spirit of untruth, lies and deception will be frustrated."

Now the Lady looks at the sheep round about Her and says, "You that stand with your head upturned, do teach those that still roam about, grazing, to lift up theirs also.

"White people, respect the rights of the black people. You should support and help one another and 'the Lady of All Nations' will be there and help you wherever you are. She is indeed the 'Co-Redemptrix, Mediatrix and Advocate.' This will be the last dogma. Set to work at it immediately and speedily. 'The Lady of All Nations' promises to aid mankind if they acknowledge this title and invoke Her under this title. Make this message known. It is high time! Fear not, I will help.

"This picture will go to the Netherlands, to Amsterdam, and that in the year '53. It will be placed in the new church – the Church of 'the Lady of All Nations.' It will be entrusted to the care of the Dominicans and temporarily be brought into a chapel or church, the choice of which is left to the clergy and the donor of the painting. The new church must be built as quickly as possible. This picture is to be placed on the altar built on the Gospel side. On the Epistle side there will be the altar of the Father, the Son and the Holy Spirit.

Where the grass is still growing, there 'the Lady of All Nations' is soon going to be. Tell your Bishop that it is the wish of 'the Lady of All Nations' that this church should be built there. The Dominicans are to take charge of the spreading of the Messages and of the picture."

As the Lady disappears, She says, "I shall bestow great graces under this title."

FORTY-FIFTH APPARITION – 20th MARCH, 1953

I see 'the Lady of All Nations' standing before me. She says, "Tell them that the time has *now* come. It is upon us – the time, when the world will know that I have come as 'the Lady of All Nations.' I wish that now to be made known to the world. Tell the Sacristan of the Pope, that my message to him is: fear nothing. He should read all the messages and pass them on to the Holy Father. Do not fear child. You will get there. Have no fear. It is I who gave you the message that the time has come."

After a long pause the Lady adds, "53 is the year of 'the Lady of All Nations.'"

Now the Lady looks in front of Her for a long time and finally says, "Before the Lord Jesus Christ returned to the Father – before the Sacrifice of the Cross began – the Lord Jesus Christ gave to the nations of the whole world the daily miracle." Now the Lady casts a searching glance over the globe and very slowly and questioningly says, "How many are there...(pause) who experience this great wonder? They pass this great miracle by. The daily Sacrifice has to have its place again at the center of this degenerate world."

Then the Lady seems to look into the distance, saying, "And now I address myself to the Holy Father: you have accomplished much. Now 'the Lady of All Nations' asks you once again to make sure to see *everything through* that remains to be done. He knows what I mean. The Holy Father should prepare the Marian dogma of the Co-Redemptrix, Mediatrix and Advocate. She will do Her part in it."

Now there is a an extremely long pause while the Lady looks searchingly into the distance. Then She says, "In order to prove that I am 'the Lady of All Nations,' I said: great powers will be overthrown; a politico-economic struggle will arise; be on your guard against false prophets; be on the lookout for the meteors; there will be disaster; there will be catastrophes of nature. We are faced with weighty decisions. – We shall be under heavy pressure."

Then the Lady gazes in front of Her as if into an abyss and says very slowly and distinctly. "53. Peoples of Europe , close your ranks. It is 'the Lady of All Nations' who calls on you to do so – *not as though you would want to destroy your enemy, but so that you might win him over to your side. Just as you are striving to achieve political unity, so you must also be of one mind in the True, Holy Spirit.* A great sense of oppression hangs over the world. Your enemy is lying in wait. Church of Rome, seize your opportunity. It is the modern humanism, realism, socialism and communism that have the world in their clutches. Listen to the Lady who wants to be your Mother.

"Pray, nations, that your sacrifice may be acceptable to the Lord. Pray, nations, that 'the Lady of All Nations' may be your Advocate."

Then the Lady, very slowly and distinctly, adds, "And now 'the Lady of All Nations' promises to grant *true peace* to all nations. *But* the nations, *together with* the Church – understand well – together *with* the Church will have to say My prayer in that year. Inform the Sacristan. Tell him that *this* is the time for it. Great world events are still to come."

The Lady has stopped speaking and seems to be moving from Her place. Then She adds, "Watch where I am going." (Now I see the Lady as it were, standing near the 'Wandelweg' in Amsterdam, above a plot of grass). "You see Me standing here in the field. This is where the new church is going to be."

I seem to be entering the church with Her. Then the Lady speaks: "On the High Altar the Sacrifice of the Cross- the 'Daily Miracle.'" (I now see the High Altar and the Lady indicates the tabernacle and the crucifix), "Adjacent to it, on the Gospel side, will be the altar of 'the Lady of All Nations,' and on the Epistle side the altar of the Father, the Son and the Holy Spirit. Notice well, my child: on the same level with the Sacrifice." (Here the Lady indicates the High Altar again and I see the three altars adjoining on the same level).

The Lady continues, "I have chosen the Dominican Fathers for this task. There the donor should place the painting, which must promptly go to Amsterdam. It is Amsterdam I have selected as the seat of 'the Lady of All Nations.' This is also the City of the Blessed Sacrament. Make sure you grasp all this. The work of spreading should be taken in hand by the monasteries and thence go to all the clergy, to all the peoples. Dominicans, remember what has been given into your charge." (This the Lady says with emphasis.)

"Your director should see to it. Have no fear. It is Mary, 'the Lady of All Nations' who brings you this message." After a pause the Lady says, clearly and slowly, "She will save the world under this title."

Then the Lady very slowly disappears.

FORTY-SIXTH APPARITION – 10th MAY, 1953

The Lady is standing before me and She says, "I have come today to give you a special message: ask the Holy Father if he would kindly say, and lead all nations in saying, the prayer with Mary, the Co-Redemptrix, Mediatrix and Advocate, under the title of 'the Lady of All Nations,' which She has given to the world. Say to him: apostle of the Lord Jesus Christ, teach your people this simple, but profound prayer. It is Mary, 'the Lady of All Nations,' who is asking this of you. You are the Shepherd of the Church of the Lord Jesus Christ. Tend your sheep. Know well that great and threatening dangers are hanging over the Church, over the world. *Now* the moment has arrived, when you should speak of Mary as the Co-Redemptrix, Mediatrix, and Advocate, under the title of 'Lady of All Nations.' Why is Mary asking you to do this? It is because She is sent by Her Lord and Creator, so that, by means of this prayer and this title, She may save the world from a universal calamity. You know that Mary wishes to come as 'the Lady of All Nations.' Now She is asking you that the nations might hear this title from you, the Holy Father.

"The Sacristan of the Pope should hand on this message, like the previous ones, to the Holy Father. The Lady will save the world by means of this prayer. I repeat this promise."

Here the Lady pauses for a long time, while I see the globe rotating under Her feet. It is as though big, black clouds were hanging about it and the Lady, looking at them, says, "Now I speak to *all the nations of the world:* Pray, nations, that your sacrifice may be acceptable to the Lord. Nations, come back and try to find your simple faith. Acknowledge your Creator and be *grateful.* This is no longer to be found among mankind, a perverse spirit governs the world. A modern paganism, humanism, atheism. modern socialism and communism control the world.

"Beware of the false prophets! 'The Lady of All Nations' cannot tell you this often enough, nor warn you sufficiently, Do listen, everyone. The Lord who sends Me to warn you, is the same Lord Who once was sacrificed for mankind, today. Oh, you do not know what tremendous forces are threatening this world. I am now not speaking only of modern humanism, atheism, modern socialism and communism; there are yet forces of quite a different nature that threaten this world. Nations, do search for the *truth.* Nations, unite.

"Without your being aware of it, the Lady has kept coming for the past eight years in order to preserve you from this. 53 is the year of 'the Lady of All Nations.'

"'53 is the year in which great world events and world-wide disaster will happen and threaten. 'The Lady of All Nations,' therefore, asks you to say this prayer. Spread this prayer as much as possible.

"Now I speak to your Bishop: do let the church of 'the Lady of All Nations' be built in Amsterdam, on the site I have pointed out."

The Lady pauses for a moment, looking into the distance. Then She adds, very *distinctly* and *slowly,*

"Marian thought must become more pronounced in these times. Amsterdam will become the *focus* for 'the Lady of All Nations.' There the peoples will get to know 'the Lady of All Nations' and learn to pray to Her under this title, to obtain *unity* for themselves, *unity among the nations.* This picture will precede the last Marian dogma. The image will, in the first place, go to Amsterdam. Your director and all who can participate, will take charge of the work of spreading.

"*One* great Community has to be formed, the direction of which I place into the hands of the Dominican Fathers. Let them well consider what I entrust them with!"

During the interval I tell the Lady that I am afraid to pass on this message. Whereupon, the Lady smiles and says, "Child, do not be afraid to make it known. You are the instrument. The Lady takes care of everything."

Then I see the Lady slowly vanishing.

FORTY-SEVENTH APPARITION – 11th OCTOBER, 1953

I see the Lady standing there. She says, "Mary, 'the Lady of All Nations,' has been sent today, in order to warn the world, the Church of Rome, and all the peoples once again of degeneration, disasters and war. The world is degenerating and more disasters are yet to come. The peoples are still living in war."

Again the Lady, with that thoughtful expression, says very slowly and distinctly, "The year 53 is the year in which 'the Lady of All Nations' must be brought to the world."

For a long time the Lady stands silent, and then resumes, "'The Lady of All Nations' has the power to bring the world *peace*. Yet She has to be asked for it under *this title*. 'The Lady of All Nations' will assist the Church of Rome. The Church of Rome – the Community – should invoke Mary, the Mother of the Lord Jesus Christ, under the new title: 'the Lady of All Nations.' They should say My *prayer* against degeneration, disaster and war, and spread it among all peoples. I shall help the Church of Rome – the Community. The nations should call on Me under *this* title."

A thoughtful silence follows. Then the Lady says with emphasis, "The Lord is the Redeemer of all nations. Mary, the Mother, was from the *beginning chosen* as Co-Redemptrix. She *became* Co-Redemptrix at the departure of the Lord Jesus Christ to the Father. She became the Mediatrix and Advocate of all people."

The Lady now waits for a moment and then continues, "Because Mary was destined to be the Co-Redemptrix, Mediatrix and Advocate, She comes *now* into *these times*, as 'the Lady of All

Nations.' Because Mary will be given the title of 'the Lady of All Nations,' She has come under this title in different places, in different countries."

With a thoughtful expression the Lady then says, "The Lady, who must bring *peace*, came and gave Her prayer in the country where Satan had reigned. The Lady, who is bringing peace, gave Her words through an instrument from a country, where peace was always desired. 'The Lady of All Nations' is not destined for *one* country and *one* place, but is meant for the whole world, for all nations. This picture will go to Amsterdam, however, and that at the end of '53. It will be placed in a chapel or church. Later, it will be transferred to the church of 'the Lady of All Nations.'

"My directions for this I have already given and they should be strictly adhered to. 'The Lady of All Nations' has a few more messages to give. Her time is almost at an end."

After a moment's silence the Lady continues very distinctly and slowly, "Then the great work will begin – the crowning of Mary, the proclamation of the dogma of the Co-Redemptrix, Mediatrix and Advocate. First, however, let the Church and the nations invoke Mary under the new title and say *Her* prayer so that degeneration, disasters and wars may be staved off from this world. If they *do* this, the peoples of Europe will heave a sigh of relief after '54."

Now the Lady casts Her eyes over the globe on which She stands, saying, "Then the world's great task will come." The Lady looks about Her and pointing to the sheep, says, "Look at My *black* sheep: White sheep, *beware!* Now there is yet time for you all to co-operate in order to achieve unity.

"Church of Rome, 'the Lady of All Nations' will only come a few times more. She keeps on warning against false prophets. Ponder the messages the Lady has given you. Sacristan of the Pope, hand these messages on."

Now, lifting up Her index finger as if in warning, the Lady says, "Holy Father, you have a great task to fulfill before you will be received among Us. Again I exhort you: do carry out the plans you have drawn up. See to the last dogma – the crowning of the Mother of the Lord Jesus Christ, the Co-Redemptrix, Mediatrix, and Advocate. In '54, you are to announce this new title to the nations. Let your care extend to the countries in which the Lord Jesus Christ is persecuted. This *can* and *shall* become a great world movement, at the head of which Mary will stand as 'the Lady of All Nations.' I shall help. I shall, through My Lord, be able to heal the nations."

Then the finger goes down again and the Lady, resuming Her well known attitude, waits a little before She adds, "And now I speak to your Bishop: you should *understand* why I speak to the Holy Father and his Sacristan. This movement is not for *one* country only, but for *all* nations. Do your part in your own country, however, for the spread of the prayer and these messages. Mary takes the responsibility. You know She said that the painting would be placed under the care of the Dominican Fathers. You know that She said the donations should not be used only for the Dominicans, but for *all the needs of the church* as well. Introduce Mary as 'the Lady of All Nations' into your country. There the great world movement will originate. The time has *now* come and it is very short. Mary stands here as the Mother who wants to help Her children. Ask and She will help you – under this new title."

Now the Lady disappears slowly.

FORTY-EIGHTH APPARITION - 3rd DECEMBER, 1953

While I am praying before the picture, I suddenly see the Lady as if She stepped out of the painting, and I hear Her say, clearly and earnestly. "Fear nothing. It was my intention that at the beginning of the Marian Year, My picture should still be here (in Germany). After that it will go to Amsterdam."

The Lady waits a moment and then says, "The powers of hell will break loose. But they will not prevail against 'the Lady of All Nations.'" While She spoke these words, I saw a brilliant light radiating from Her in all directions.

FORTY-NINTH APPARITION - 4th APRIL, 1954

I see the Lady standing with a serious look on Her face. She says to me, "Once more I am here. Listen well: from the outset the Handmaid of the Lord was chosen to be Co-Redemptrix. Tell your theologians that they can find it all in their books!"

The Lady pauses briefly, then smiling to Herself, She says, almost in a whisper, "I am not bringing a new doctrine. I am *now* bringing *old* ideas."

She waits and then continues, "Because the Lady is Co-Redemptrix, She is also Mediatrix and Advocate; not only because She is the Mother of the Lord Jesus Christ, but – and mark this well – , because She is the Immaculate Conception.

"Theologians, I ask you, do you *still* have objections to this dogma? You can find these words and ideas. I ask you to *work* for this dogma. No, fear nothing! There will be a clash. The other indeed will attack you; but the simplicity of this dogma lies in these last thoughts which Mary, 'the Lady of All Nations,' puts before you today. *Do fight and ask for this dogma:* it is the crowning of *your Lady!"* (The Lady says this emphasis on almost every word.) Then She gazes in front of Her for quite a while with a peculiar expression on Her face as if She looked into the distance, and says, "The Lady, the Handmaid of the Lord, was chosen and made fruitful by the Holy Spirit."

The Lady pauses and says very slowly, "The Lady was *chosen.* She was also to be present at the Descent of the Holy Spirit. The Holy Spirit had to come down upon the Apostles. – (and raising Her finger, She adds with emphasis) the *first* theologians! For this reason the Lord willed that His Mother should be present there. *His Mother,* 'the Lady of All Nations,' became at the departure of Her Son, 'the Lady of All Nations,' the Co-Redemptrix, Mediatrix and Advocate, in the presence of one Apostle, *one* theologian, to be witness to it. For he had to take care of 'thy Mother.' She had to take care of 'Her Apostles.'"

Now the Lady looks at me and says with emphasis. "This is the last time that the Lady speaks about *this dogma.* She will return, but for other matters.

"Tell your theologians, however, that now they have everything in their hands. *Now* they have to accomplish the Will of the Lord Jesus Christ. Tell the theologians that 'the Lady of All Nations' will see to its fulfillment."

Now the Lady spreads Her hands as if in protection over something. Then She says, "I will stand by the Holy Father. Mark My words well. He will be given the necessary strength to get everything ready. – Many changes are ahead." (And now I clearly see the Lady, so to say, standing above St. Peter's, while everything seems to be spinning around). Then She says, "Let the Holy Father carry out his splendid plan as quickly as he possibly can! Tell him that 'the Lady of All Nations' has helped him and will give him all the strength he needs. The Holy Father knows all that is necessary. What he lacks in vigour, the Lady will give him. He know what he has."

Now the hands of the Lady return to their usual position and She adds with emphasis, "Tell the Sacristan that everything is going to come right. He should act and persevere as the Lady desires of him."

Now the Lady looks at me again with a smile and, moving Her finger to and fro, says, "Now to your Bishop: You should request him to make the prayer and the messages known." (I tell the Lady that he will not do so and I am so frightened at having to tell him again.)

The Lady looks at me seemingly in compassion and with a smile, says, "Do not be afraid, child, ask him quite simply. Tell him, *this* is the given moment. He can accept the prayer as coming from Me. He can consent to the building of the church. My signs are inherent in My words; tell him that. Tell him also that the Lady wishes Her picture to be exposed to the public *now* and add, moreover, that the prayer comes from 'his Mother Mary' who wishes also to be his 'Lady of All Nations.' Tell him: Mary takes full responsibility. Later, I shall give more signs, when My words shall cease. I shall come back and speak to the nations. All this had to come first."

Then the Lady looks in front of Her earnestly and it is as though I see heavy clouds surging around the globe on which She stands, while the globe is rotating fast. The Lady points at the globe and says very sadly, "Look to the world – mark well what I am going to tell you." At this, the Lady holds up Her right hand and lets me look into it.

I see in it a large die and the Lady moves Her hand as though shaking it over the world. Then She says, "Satan's hand goes all over the world, holding a die. Do you know, Church – Community – what this means? Satan is still the prince of this world. He keeps his grasp on everything he can. That then is *why* 'the Lady of All

Nations' had to come *now*, into *these* times. For She is the Immaculate Conception and, therefore, also the Co-Redemptrix, Mediatrix and Advocate. These three concepts in one.

"Theologians, have you heard this aright? The Lady was bound to bring Her prayer over this diabolical world. For the Holy Spirit has still to descend upon the nations. Understand this message well. Say My prayer, then, nations, that the Holy Spirit *will really* and *truly* come."(At this last sentence Mary held Her hand aloft, as if showing the people how to pray.)

The Lady waits again and looks very seriously at me, yet with a smile. She says, "And you, child, are you afraid to pass on all this? Then the Lady says to you: let them come with all their needs – spiritual and bodily alike – the Lady is here, in readiness. She will bring them *back* and *will help* them. Make a sacrifice of your life. Tell your director that the Lord always chooses the weak for His great designs. Let him be a ease!"

Now the Lady, looking far away, says, "And to *all* the others, I say, *work on;* fight for 'the Lady of All Nations;' She *has* to come at this time! I will help them. – I shall return on May 31st."

Then the Lady disappears very slowly.

FIFTIETH APPARITION—31st MAY, 1954
(The person addressed was unaware that the Feast of "Mary, Mediatrix of All Graces" was kept on that date.)

"Once more I am here. — The Co-Redemptrix, Mediatrix and Advocate is now standing before you. I have chosen this day: on this day the Lady will be crowned. Theologians and apostles of the Lord Jesus Christ, listen carefully: I have given you the explanation of the dogma. Work and ask for this dogma. You should petition the Holy Father for this dogma. The Lord Jesus Christ has wrought great things and will give even more to you all in these times, in this twentieth century. On this date 'the Lady of All Nations' will receive Her official title of 'Lady of All Nations.' Note well: these *three concepts* in one. These three. (at this the Lady puts up three fingers and moves the other hand round about Her until She becomes as it were enveloped in a delicate mist). Now I have demonstrated *these three* concepts to your theologians. These three concepts as one whole. I am saying this twice because there are some who will accept only *one* concept. The Holy Father will agree to the former. But you will have to help him to achieve this. Make no mistake about it."

And of a sudden, it is as if I was standing with the Lady over the dome of a big church and as we enter, I hear the Lady say, "I am taking you inside this. Tell others what I let you see and hear." *We* are now in a very big church, in St. Peter's. I see lots of cardinals and bishops. The Pope enters. He is being carried in a kind of chair. People applaud. The choir begins to sing. Now the Holy Father is announcing something, while holding up two fingers. Then all at once the Lady is standing on the globe again and says with a smile, "In this way, my child, I have let you see what is the Will of the Lord Jesus Christ. This day will in due time, be the 'Coronation Day' of His Mother, 'the Lady of All Nations,' who once was Mary." Here the Lady pauses, gazing into the distance. After a while, She says, "The Lady remained with Her apostles until the Spirit came.

"In the same way, the Lady will come to Her apostles and all the nations, in order to bring them the Holy Spirit *anew*. Because— the Holy Spirit of Truth must always be invoked before great decisions."

Again the Lady waits a while and then says in a low voice, "My prophecy, 'From henceforth all generations shall call Me blessed,' will be fulfilled more than ever before, once the dogma has been proclaimed. The Holy Father knows his time. He will prepare it and accomplish it before he will be taken up to dwell with Us. On that day, all nations will call Me blessed. I have come on this day so that they (and She points around Her) may bear witness that 'the Lady of All Nations' has *really* and *truly* said this.

"I have said: Church of Rome, I shall come only a few times more. By this 'the Lady of All Nations' wished to say: only a few more times before the proclamation of the dogma. Do watch out for that. And here is My *sign:* 'the Lady of All Nations' is allowed to come under this title every year to Her children, to Her apostles, to all nations."

"I manifested Myself to the world in different ways. (The Lady looks at the globe, points out places where She appeared in the past and shakes Her head very sadly). Now I ask: has it availed (effected) anything?

"The Lord Jesus Christ has yet one more favour to grant to the world, which is: the *word,* the *voice* of His Mother, 'the Lady of All Nations.' By means of this instrument, in a small country that is on the edge of the precipice, 'the Lady of All Nations' will give Her motherly admonitions and consolations every year. Later on, this will *cease.* My child, they will believe you.

"Look, I am with you... I shall be your support and help. The picture must be placed in public. Petition your Bishop. He should consent to have the picture exposed to the public. He should consent to the erection of the church I have shown you. Let all fight for it! Tell your director. I will help him and likewise the *others.* It is *My* prayer, tell your Bishop. He should give his consent. No, child, do not be afraid."

Now the Lady looks in front of Her for a moment before She resumes, "From now on all nations will call Me blessed. 'The Lady of All Nations' desires unity in the Holy Spirit of Truth. The world is encompassed by a false spirit—*Satan.* When the dogma, the last dogma in Marian history, has been proclaimed, 'the Lady of All Nations' will give *peace, true peace* to the world. The nations, however, must say My prayer in union with the Church. They must know that 'the Lady of All Nations' has come as Co-Redemptrix, Mediatrix and Advocate. So be it!

"I shall return, as I have promised today, but then in public.— No, child, do not be afraid. So be it!"

Then the Lady stands in silence for a long time before She continues, "Now I am speaking to the nations of the entire world: apostles and nations all, kneel down before you Lord and Creator and be *thankful.* Science today has made people forget to show *gratitude.* They no longer recognize their Creator. Nations, be warned, bow down in deep humility before your Creator. Implore His mercy; He is merciful. Is He not giving you every proof of it in these times? The Father, the Son and the Holy Spirit be with you all the days of your lives! May the Father and the Son give you 'the Lady of All Nations!' Whoever or Whatever you are, I can be to you 'the Mother, the Lady of All Nations.' See to it, nations, that those who are in need—and by this I also mean *spiritual* need—be brought to the Lady. Go to work among others with *My prayer.*"

After a short pause She says, "The Lady will return every year." And then She slowly disappears.

FIFTY-FIRST APPARITION—31st MAY 1955

(During Benediction in the church of St. Thomas Aquinas.) The Lady says, "Say My prayer." But because of emotion I am unable to say the prayer at once. Then the Lady says again, "Say My prayer," and She Herself starts prompting the prayer: "Lord Jesus Christ..." and makes me continue it.

Now the Lady waits a short while, looks in front of Her and then begins to speak, "I am standing here as 'the Lady of All Nations,' the Co-Redemptrix, Mediatrix and Advocate..."

Here the Lady breaks off; then, as if addressing an invisible crowd in front of Her, begins to speak as follows: "I have promised to come today, 31st May. The Mother, 'the Lady of All Nations,' is standing here before you. She wants to address the nations today. Listen carefully to my words... I have come to warn the nations: Satan is not yet banished.

"Nations, be warned against the false prophets. 'The Lady of All Nations' *is allowed* to come every year. She promised to give Her sign — this sign has now been given...I said: I shall come back, but in a public place. Well, then, nations, this instrument hears the voice of the Lady, so that she may convey Her word to you."

Here the Lady waits a while, then says, "Satan is not banished yet. 'The Lady of All Nations' is *now* permitted to come in order to banish Satan. She comes to announce the Holy Spirit. The Holy Spirit will only *now* descend over this earth. But you should say My prayer, the one I gave to the world. Every day and every moment *you* should think of the prayer 'the Lady of All Nations' gave to this world at *this* time.

"How thoroughly Satan holds the world in his clutches, only God knows. He *now* sends to you , to all the nations, His Mother, 'the Lady of All Nations.' She will vanquish Satan, as has been foretold. She shall place Her foot upon Satan's head.

"Nations, do not be deceived by false prophets, listen only to HIM, to GOD, the Father, the Son and the Holy Spirit. For the same... Father... is the same... Son (very slowly and with pauses). — The same... Father and Son... is the same... Holy Spirit."

Then the Lady waits a long time and says, "You will have to endure a great deal as yet in this century. You, nations of this era, do realize that you are under the protection of 'the Lady of All Nations;' call upon Her as the Advocate; ask Her to stave off all disasters; ask Her to banish degeneration from this world.

"Degeneration breeds disaster. Degeneration generates war. You should ask by means of My prayer to eject it from this world; you do not know what great value and power this prayer boasts before God! He will grant the requests of His Mother, when She comes to plead for you as Advocate."

Here the Lady waits a long time before She goes on: "Great events are impending. You, young people, will see enormous changes; it is 'the Lady of All Nations' who tells you this. She will protect you. She will reign in this age...in *this age,* in *this world* — over all nations, as the Lady. This will be a time of stupendous and awesome inventions; so that even your pastors will stand amazed and will tell you: we too are at our wits' end. Then take to heart the words the Lady spoke to you on May 31st. The *Father* knows, and permits, all that will come and pass in the world.

"Know well that the Holy Spirit is nearer than ever. The Holy Spirit will come *now* only, if you pray for His coming. He has always been ready; now, however, the time has come.

"The world has lost its bearings? Well then, nations, put your trust in your Mother, who has never yet forsaken Her children. She is allowed to come to you under this *new* title: Co-Redemptrix, Mediatrix and Advocate.

"Why do you not ask your Holy Father to pronounce the dogma the Lady demands?" (The Lady pauses during the Benediction of the Blessed Sacrament. The Lady joins Her hands together for a moment, while before and after this, Her hands are extended as in the picture. Directly the blessing is over, She continues), "Once the dogma has been pronounced, 'the Lady of All Nations' will give Her blessing...*Then* 'the Lady of All Nations' will bestow peace. She will help you when this dogma has been proclaimed.

"Great things are about to happen. The world is in the throes of degeneration. Nations, be mindful of the daily miracle given to you by the Lord Jesus Christ. He gave it to you, so that you might experience it every day. Do you realize what it is you are going without?

"Nations, I told you I would come to summon the peoples and bring succour to my children — the apostles and all the nations. Well, the Lady has *now* come.

"You must lead your children to the Lord Jesus Christ; you must teach them again how to pray, just as 'the Lady of All Nations' teaches you to say Her prayer. The Lady asks you, parents, to teach your children this prayer. Bring your children back to the Sacrifice. Let all nations come back to the Sacrifice!

"And when I say 'nations,' I mean thereby My white and especially My black sheep, standing about Me. White people, do concern yourselves with the black peoples; they have to be led towards the Lord Jesus Christ; they have to be shown the way to the Father, the Son and the Holy Spirit.

"When you begin to ask the Holy Father for the dogma, the Lady will fulfill Her promise and true peace will come. *True peace,* nations, that is the kingdom of God. God's kingdom now is nearer than ever. Understand these words well.

"It is really and truly the Mother, 'the Lady of All Nations,' who is telling you this. Here then is My admonition: do not listen to false prophets. Listen only to your shepherds, to those who lead you the right way, to the voice of conscience... to a 'Higher Being"— this I say for the benefit of those who do not belong to the true Church.

"You, members of the Church of Rome, appreciate your great, *your own great* happiness. Realize what it means to belong to the Church of Rome! Do your actions bear this out? Your Mother, 'the Lady of All Nations,' may come to you once a year under this new title; later this will change. Understand My words well when I say: make sure that every year the nations will be assembled around this throne, before this picture. This is the great favour that Mary, 'Miriam' or 'the Lady of All Nations' is allowed to bestow on the world.

"I said: She will come back; She will speak to Her apostles. Now the Lady is addressing you first: all you, nations, stand by your apostles; do not make things so difficult for them. Offer your children again as a sacrifice to the Lord. Apostles of the Lord Jesus Christ, your Lady understands you, your Lady will help you in all your difficulties; your Lady will assist you. In Her name ask the Father, the Son and the Holy Spirit, who will come now more fully than ever.

"The kingdom of God is nearer than ever. Nations, do you realize what that will mean? Are you aware, nations, that the responsibility lies *on you*? You, men who hold higher positions in this world, do not lead your children astray ; do not misguide the least of My children; you are responsible before your Lord Jesus Christ (and the Lady repeats with emphasis), *you bear the responsibility.*

"I said a minute ago: alarming inventions will be made. God permits this; but you, nations, can make sure that it does not result in disaster.

"Nations— I implore you — the Lady *entreats* you; mark it well: the Mother of God has never entreated you in this way before."

Now the Lady waits again before She says, "To spare you from falling a prey to alarming inventions, nations, *the Lady begs you now, today,* do ask the Father, the Son and the Holy Spirit that He may protect His people and may restore unity among them. Unity is what His people must achieve, they must be *one*, and over them, 'the Lady of All Nations.' One Community, nations, I stress these words: *One Community!*

"Take thought of the future. (and now the Lady seems to smile). No..., the Lady does *not* say: provide for your *material* future. Try to understand the reason of My coming on this day. The Lord Jesus Christ has selected this great day for 'the Lady of All Nations.'

"Her mission is to establish unity among Her nations. She is sent to make *one* great Community of Her nations. To gather all nations into *one* Community, that is the task set before the world in this present time, which I have heralded repeatedly. Again and again, I have spoken of this time in private. Well now, this time has come.

"Satan is not banished yet — it is for you to see to that, you, people of the Church of Rome. Remember your Sacraments; they *still* exist! You, Christian people, by your example bring others to Him, to the daily Miracle, to the daily Sacrifice.

"In this way the words; 'From henceforth all generations shall call me blessed,' will be fulfilled. Today this message of 'the Lady of All Nations' goes out over the world. I said, 'I will comfort you.' Nations, your Mother knows what life is like; your Mother is familiar with sorrow. Your Mother knows what the Cross means. Whatever you suffer in this life, your Mother, 'the Lady of All Nations,' suffered before you. She has shown you the way in Her own person." The Lady waits a moment and adds very slowly, "But She went up to the Father, She returned to Her Son. You too, nations, go to the Father along the way of the Cross; you too go to the Son along the same way of the Cross; the Holy Spirit will help you to do this. Implore Him now. I cannot repeat this often enough to the world: *have recourse to the Holy Spirit now.*" (The Lady said this very slowly, stressing every word).

"You will obtain help. Go back to the Church. Return to the Community. Look after My other sheep, those that go about, intent only on pasture.

"Do you know what that signifies — going about for pasture only? (This too the Lady said with emphasis). Above all, strive for unity among the nations. That is what 'the Lady of All Nations' has come to tell you today. She will not forget you. You are as yet unable to appreciate My words.

"'My signs' — I said — 'are inherent in my words.' Your mother will comfort you. When the time of the Lord Jesus Christ has come, you will see that false prophets, war, discord and dissension's, will disappear. Now the time is ushered in. 'The Lady of All Nations' is saying this."

Then the Lady slowly disappears.

FIFTY-SECOND APPARITION — 31st MAY, 1956

(Feast of Corpus Christi, 10 p.m., in the home of the seeress). A bright light is coming, from which the Lady slowly steps forward. She stands there and says, "For the sake of these here (the Lady points to the circle) I have come today. Indeed, I tell you, the Lord Jesus Christ has sent 'the Lady of All Nations' here because of the promise. Inform your Bishop of this. Tell your spiritual director."

Now the Lady looks at me with a smile and says, "You have acted well. Obedience was your first duty."

Here the Lady stops briefly and then says, "I had told you to go to the 'Wandelweg.'" (This the Lady had ordered me to do exactly at 3 p.m., upon which I had answered: "I cannot do this. I have to obey Father Frehe to whom I have given my word of honour").

Then the Lady, smiling at me, says, "You have obeyed. So be it. This is what the Lord has wanted of you."

After a moment's pause, looking into the distance, the Lady says, "For the sake of the town — let them take hold of My meaning — for the sake of the town, the Lady has exacted this obedience."

Now the Lady waits a good while and then, looking around as if deep in thought, she says, "Now in the presence of these witnesses, the Lady will show you where the church of 'the Lady of All Nations' is going to be and what it will look like!"

For a long time the Lady again says nothing until we suddenly seem to stand on a meadow. "Look carefully," says the Lady. Then, pointing to the right, She adds, "Not there, but on this side," clearly indicating the exact spot. "I will let you see it clearly now, so that later you can tell the others."

Now I clearly see the site on the "Wandelweg," where the church is meant to be. "Look well...," says the Lady again and after a pause, "They will have difficulties — it is a large piece of land, later to be encircled by a fair-sized suburb." (The dyke had gone).

Now I suddenly see a large church before me. She says, "You see three domes on this church, a big one (pointing to it) and on either side, a smaller one." (I can now see a smaller dome on either side. The domes are green).

Then the Lady solemnly says, "We now enter the house of the Lord." Now we seem to be standing inside a big church. It is a warm church — I cannot convey my impression of it in any better way. While we are moving to the front, I notice a huge platform.

The Lady begins to speak and, pointing out everything, She says, "In the centre we have the Crucifix, the Daily Miracle (with a gesture at the tabernacle), the altar of the Sacrifice of the Cross."

Then the Lady points to the Epistle side. She joins Her hands and says most solemnly, "The altar of the Father, the Son and the Holy Spirit."

Now, pointing to the Gospel side, She says, "On this side the altar of 'the Lady of All Nations.' Look well: on the same level." The Lady points to all this again and continues, "It looks like a semi-circle" (yet I see a big semi-circle in the middle and a smaller one on either side). The Lady says, "One big semi-circle and two smaller ones adjoining. The altar of Sacrifice is in the middle and behind it is a representation of the Last Supper." The Lady points to the central altar.

Then she goes to the Epistle side and says, "There you see the Father, sitting on the globe." I now see an image of God, the Father; a Cross is standing in His right hand. Above this image there is a dove, which radiates in all directions. The Lady says, "The Cross in His hand, you see Him (as if) overshadowed by the Holy Spirit, here represented in the form of a dove, which sends out rays in all directions."

From the place on which She stands, the Lady points to the Gospel side and says, "The altar of the Lady is depicting the way in which *I shall come*." (All this I saw in sculpture, including the representation of the Lady , at which I was greatly surprised. Comparing it with the painting I thought, "This representation in sculpture is not correct.")

The Lady smiles and says, "It is not the *present picture* that you see here," and She indicated that I should follow Her. Now we go to the back of the church on the Gospel side. The Lady says, "There is the painting, (a little more to the left), *apart,* in a chapel of its own. Such was the Will of the Lord Jesus Christ. —In addition I wish to tell you that the Lady has put you to the test." Long pause. "Where the church is going to be, She will not appear. Ask whether the painting can be put back in a public place. (Here I get a glimpse of the chapel in the church of St. Thomas). Later, it will be transferred to the house of the Lord Jesus Christ." At this She indicates the church which will have to be built at some future date.

The Lady then waits a moment before She adds, "Tell them that I have now spoken for *all* nations as well. Once the painting has been brought back , the Lady will give Her blessing."—

Now the Lady waits a little, after which She says, "One answer remains yet to be given: the Lady *has spoken* and *is speaking* according to the Will of the Lord Jesus Christ, there, where He is."

She stops and then continues once more, "Did not the Lord Jesus Christ delay His great miracle (and now the Lady speaks in a soft voice and with emphasis) — that of changing water into wine — until His Mother had spoken? He intended to *perform* His miracle, but waited until His Mother had spoken. Do you see what I mean? This is My reply today to those who could not understand that the Lady should have appeared on May 31st, 1955, in the church of St. Thomas (during exposition of the Blessed Sacrament!)."

For a moment the Lady pauses, then looking in front of Her sadly, She says, "Also for those who are in error, the Lady says so. This thought should help them to form a more correct idea of the relationship of the Lady with Her Lord. Pass all this on well."

Then with a sad and thoughtful expression on Her face the Lady says, "I had wanted to bring an important and joyous message.— Ask to have the painting restored to the public."

Then the Lady slowly — very slowly — goes away.

FIFTY-THIRD APPARITION — 31st MAY, 1957
(At 3 p.m., in the church of St. Thomas)

When I entered the church, the people were saying the Rosary. After that they said the twelve articles of the Creed. At the words, "Who was conceived by the Holy Spirit," I suddenly saw the light appear close to the Lady-altar. Very slowly it moved along the church towards the chapel.

I rose and went to the chapel as well, (because the Lady as it were beckoned to me).

Then the Lady slowly emerged from the light and stood before me. She said, "Say the prayer."

I did so and the Lady prayed with me. At the end, however, I heard Her say, "your" instead of *"our" Advocate*. This confused me so that it seems I left out the words, "who once was Mary," and repeated Her "your Advocate."

Then the Lady said, "Today I have come here in order to give the last message in public. —Do not be afraid, child, it is 'the Lady of All Nations' who says all this — (pause). You have acted well." (pause...).

The Lady looked very sadly in front of Her and then said, "I *had wanted* to bring an important and joyous message. I have let it become clear to all nations that obedience and free will — yes, free will — were given precedence. *Now* I will give a reply to those who have asked for a sign." (Here the Lady compassionately shook Her head.) "To all of them I say: My signs are contained in My *words*. Oh, you of little faith! You are like children who insist upon fireworks, whereas they have no eyes for the true light and for the true fire. (Here the Lady smiled, full of compassion.)

"You seek and seek in para-this and para-that. But to this 'the Lady of All Nations' has a reply as well: it is the PARACLETE who effects all this."

(I did not know how to interpret the meaning of this word and tried to convey this to the Lady by shaking my head.) She smiled again and continued, "*You* all know what it means." (The Lady was addressing the *others* present, since She pointed round about Her).

Then the Lady said further, "He is the salt; He is the Water; He is the light; He is the power by which the Lady was overshadowed. He proceeded from the Father and the Son. He overshadowed 'the Lady of All Nations' with His power. In virtue of this, She can and does distribute grace to you.

"Go then and spread My prayer, the prayer from the Lord. Ask if the picture may be brought here *for the time being*.

"Be not afraid, child. It is I who am asking this. Petition for the dogma. And you, nations, all of you, allow yourselves to be led to the Lord, led to your Sacraments, at the hands of the Lady."

Now the Lady shakes Her head and with a strange look on Her face, She adds, "What a strange way of dealing with them you have!

"I know, 'the Lady of All Nations' *knows* what it means for *Christians* to live in these times! And, therefore, She has been allowed to come and warn you for the last twelve years —(In a split-second I ask myself whether this is correct) — to help you, to guide you *back* to the Lord Jesus Christ.

"You have experienced this year how great the power of Satan can become. The Lady of All Nations, who is the Bride of the Lord, the Queen of the King, *who has now received this title* from the Lord, She has once again saved the world by Her intercession — *once more saved it!*" Here the Lady lifts a warning finger.

"Do listen, nations, to *everything* I have said. Believe Me! —it is worth the trouble to leave the world. (I think the Lady meant this in a double sense.)

"Surely, you all have to get to *heaven!*" (This the Lady said very clearly and explicitly and it was as if She drew aside a veil and I experienced a peculiar state — a "heavenly, a supernatural" state. I saw something tremendous, quite impossible to repeat. It was as if heaven had opened, so beautiful!)

"The Lord has redeemed *all of you.* Those of you, who have gone astray, come back. The Lady is waiting for you." (At this time the Lady gestured invitingly, as though She wanted to gather all mankind in Her arms).

She said further, "She will help you. She will lead you back." Then a long pause follows...

Then the Lady, as if gazing at something, with a heavenly expression on Her face, said solemnly, "Before the Lord Jesus Christ died His bodily death; before the Lord Jesus Christ ascended to the Father; before the Lord Jesus Christ *appeared* in the world —moved anew among men —(it looked as if the Lady added this by way of explanation, because I was shaking my head, not knowing what to make of it) He gave you the great Mystery, the great Miracle of every day, every hour, every minute. He gave you *Himself.* No, nations, (She shook Her head vehemently as She said this) not merely a remembrance; no, nations, listen to what He said: not just an idea, but *Himself,* under the appearance of a little piece of bread, under the appearance of wine. This is how the Lord wants to come among you, day after day. Do accept it. Do act on it. He gives you the *foretaste,* — the foretastes of eternal life.

"This, nations, is what the Lady, the Co-Redemptrix, Mediatrix and Advocate wanted to tell you today, at the last appearance in a public place."

Then I see the Lady slowly disappearing.

FIFTY-FOURTH APPARITION
18th-19th FEBRUARY, 1958
Ash Wednesday, 19th February, 1958

Last night I woke up again with a start, because I was called at three o' clock precisely. I saw the light again and heard the voice of the Lady say, "Once more I am here. The peace of the Lord Jesus Christ be with you! You have acted well; you have chosen from free will to bring the message to your spiritual director. This obedience will bear good fruit, which you will experience in a short time. Your spiritual director knows his duty. You may be at ease. I shall make a communication to you, which you must keep secret from everybody, (including the Sacristan and your director). When it has happened, you may inform them that the Lady *now* told you this.

"The communication is: This Holy Father, Pope Pius XII, will at the beginning of October of this year be taken up to dwell with Us. The Lady of All Nations, the Co-Redemptrix, Mediatrix and Advocate will lead him to everlasting bliss." (I was very frightened at this communication and dared hardly believe it).

The Lady said, "Do not be frightened, child. His successor will pronounce the dogma."

I thanked the Lady and She said very solemnly, "AMEN."

FIFTY-FIFTH APPARITION — 31st MAY, 1958
(11:50-12:10, noon.)

We were sitting together, conversing quietly, when all at once I saw a strong light appear in the adjacent room. The Lady I did not see.

Then it was as if a veil was lifted before my eyes and I experienced a "heavenly, a supernatural" state. What I saw, I am wholly unable to express. It was — if in all humility I may say so — something "heavenly." This remained before my eyes until I suddenly saw the Lady, but far away. She spoke to me very softly, I could not repeat Her words — I had no voice.

The Lady said, "Through the Lord to the Lady; through 'the Lady of All Nations' to the Lord of All Nations. — The contact will remain. Warn the clergy against heretical doctrines, particularly in the domain of the Eucharist. Convey this to the Sacristan. Tell him that the Lady asks him to bring you to the Supreme Pastor. I repeat: pray much *for priests*, for an *increase* of good priests, and for the conversion of the nations. But!..."

Suddenly, the Lady stopped and made a gesture with Her head as if She wanted to say, "Listen, repeat my words." All at once I recovered my voice. She said,

"In all tranquillity I came; in all tranquillity I shall return to Him, Who sent Me." (This made me very sad.) The Lady continued, *"Do not be sad. I do not leave you orphans. —He, the COM-*FORTER and HELPER *will come."* The Lady then disappeared slowly and I heard Her say, "Listen, follow the light."

All at once the light had gone out of the room. I sought it in the next, but it went before me to the door of our house. I hurried after it (along the street) and it led me to the "Wandelweg." There it suddenly stood still. I was searching on the ground when I heard the voice say, *"What are you looking for?"*

The voice came from above. I looked up and must have said aloud: "Oh, there She is!"

Then I saw the Lady (with Cross, globe and sheep) between two clouds, standing against a background of radiant, blue sky. As She was very slowly moving upwards, I heard Her say,

"This is the site of my return to Him. Here build one Community for all Nations." Now a big, shining cloud enveloped Her and I saw Her no more. While She was yet going up in a haze, there came (I cannot express it otherwise), in Her place, a large Sacred Host, irradiating light. It was very large. Three shafts of rays emanated from the Sacred Host: in the centre a beam of magnificent colours; to the left and right, beams of wonderful, brilliant light. At the end of the right one, there was a Cross and at the end of the left one a Dove, but shining, symbolic, "Spiritual" I should call it. Then everything faded away.

FIFTY-SIXTH APPARITION — 31st MAY, 1959
Sunday, 31st May, from about 14:45- 15:15 p.m.

From my window I suddenly saw something happening in the air over the "Wandelweg." I was amazed and shouted to my relations, "Look! There!" pointing into the air. Then I noticed that the light stood there, a powerful light. I could not look into it and covered my eyes with my hands. Yet I was compelled to look at it. It seemed as if the sky was torn apart — it really was a tearing apart of the sky! Then I suddenly saw, in all Her glory — the Lady!

I cannot possible describe this heavenly, powerful, splendid sight. Never before had I seen Her like that. I saw no sheep, no Cross, only the Lady, but with rays of dazzling glory about Her!

Then I had suddenly to look at Her head and I saw that She wore a crown. That I had never seen before. I saw no gold or diamonds, yet I knew very well that it was a crown; for it sparkled with light all around, more brilliantly than the rarest diamonds. The Lady Herself was one blaze of light. Again — it was heavenly, glorious! Better I cannot explain myself.

Then below this splendid view, I saw a piece of thin, blue sky and underneath, the upper side of the globe. This was completely black. Then I saw the Lady moving Her finger from side to side and shaking Her head as if in disapproval and warning at the blackness of the world. And I heard Her say, "Do penance."

Then I saw something very strange happen. From out of the dark, black world, there emerged a great variety of human heads. It looked as if they were slowly moving higher, until they all at once stood on the world's hemisphere. I examined them, thinking, "I never knew that there were so many races and divisions of men."

Then I saw the Lady extending Her hands in blessing over these people, and She no longer looked quite so sad. I heard Her say, "Make reparation to Him."

Suddenly, the Lady had gone. In Her stead, I saw a big Host. It was exceedingly large and so I could see quite well that it was a normal Host, one like those we see in church, a wafer.

Then in front of the Host, there appeared a chalice. I saw that the chalice was of splendid gold. It toppled over, facing me. Then

I saw flowing from this chalice thick streams of blood. All this blood poured upon the globe and spilled over the earth; it was a distressing sight; I began to feel quite sick, all the time streams and streams of blood!

This went on for quite a while. Then the scene suddenly changed and all of it became a brilliant, dazzling Sacred Host. It shone so brightly that I shaded my eyes so as not to get blinded, but I was forced to keep looking at it. The Host seemed to be made of white fire. In the centre of it was a little opening or hollow; I cannot describe it any better. Then all of a sudden, the Host seemed to burst open, and exposed to my view was a figure, soaring in mid-air, a person, exceedingly mighty and strong.

Forgive me, please, I cannot convey the strength and majesty this person embodied, it was too overwhelming! I hardly dared look. I saw *one* person, but the thought kept recurring in my mind, "And yet there are two," and then when I looked, I saw only one. Still my mind kept repeating, "And yet there are two."

All at once there came from the two an indescribable light and in it I saw, breaking out from the centre, —I cannot express it otherwise —a Dove! It shot like an arrow down to the earth, unspeakably bright; and I covered my eyes again so as not to get blind. My eyes hurt me and yet again I was forced to keep them open and look at the vision! What splendour, what magnificence! the soaring figure, majestic, powerful, grand; and the world now all bathed in light from the radiant Dove! And a voice rang out, "He who eats and drinks Me receives life eternal and the Spirit of Truth."

When I had gazed at all this for a time, the Lady came back, arrayed in Her former glory, exactly as at the beginning. Now, however, I clearly saw the difference between Her magnificence, if I may say so, and the grandeur and majesty of the soaring figure.

Now the Lady looked happy and I heard Her say very softly in the distance, "Good-bye."

This made me very sad. I begin to weep, for I saw everything slowly fading from my sight.

REMAINING "CONTACT":

EUCHARISTIC EXPERIENCES

17th July, 1958

As I was in church this morning and followed the preparations for Holy Mass, something very strange happened to my eyes. I naturally had them open, as I was watching the altar. And yet it was as though my eyes suddenly jumped open. I cannot express myself better. I also felt it physically.

Then I saw the priest and the altar disappear as in a mist in the background.

A very bright light now appeared before my eyes. In that light I saw three figures linked with each other in a semicircle. These were of extreme whiteness — white fire I would almost call it. It startled me, for I could not look at it. I placed my hands before my eyes and really thought "I am going blind." Yet interiorly, I was impelled to keep on looking and so I did.

Then something very peculiar took place: the three figures expanded slowly, becoming larger and larger, until they formed a semi-circle. After this they joined together to form a circle. The centre still appeared as a dark patch.

Subsequently, the figures spread out towards the center. Now only a tiny spot remained dark. Suddenly that spot too was filled, so that all at once a very great sphere of white fire stood before my eyes. I cannot express it otherwise.

I looked at it; all of a sudden I recognized the Sacred Host, such as I had seen it on May 31, 1958, but without shafts of rays. I could scarcely look at it and a most peculiar state came over me.

Thus it stayed before my eyes and I kept gazing. It was white fire — magnificent!

Then it seemed as if the Sacred Host slowly faded away and the High Altar as well as the Lady-Altar were bathed in a beautiful light. That lasted for a moment.

Suddenly, everything appeared again as usual, as it had been when I entered the church. The priest meanwhile had arrived at the Epistle.

11th March, 1959

Immediately after the Credo I saw the altar bathed in an immensely bright light. The priest and the altar retreated into the background and I saw nothing but light. From it emerged, in the air above the altar, three figures, framed by a faint, circular outline, just as I had seen them the year before on July 17th, 1958, in the same place.

Everything now proceeded as then: the light hurt and I thought I would be blinded. My shock was so great that I thought my heart would stop. Again, I saw these three figures expanding until they formed a circle. Then they filled up the central space, leaving only one tiny dark spot.

But now came the difference: suddenly I saw something burst asunder within that dark spot and it was as if I saw in that great shining circle two heavenly, divine Figures (forgive my presumption); and yet it was but one Figure with outspread arms. I kept on seeing two, whereas it was just one. It was something so brilliant and heavenly that I hardly dared look and yet I had to. The Figure was floating, I would say, and fully ablaze of light, but I could not see any source of light.

Thus I sat gazing at it. Then it seemed as though something was breaking away from the two Figures and all at once I saw a Dove emerge from one of the hands, wholly of light and emitting rays. On the other side, a Cross appeared at shoulder level. All that remained before me, I do not know for how long.

Then all of a sudden, everything became a ball or circle of white fire and I saw — or better still, I thought I saw again — a shining Sacred Host.

(When I left the church, everything in the street looked dark to me, although the sun was shining and the sky was a radiant blue. My eyes were still paining me from the light. Once again — I really did see that with my eyes. And what I felt at that moment, I cannot describe. I was in fear and dread and yet not really — simply overawed.) After the vision, the church bore its usual look again. I saw the priest and the altar as before. Just the bell rang for Holy Communion.

30th August, 1959

I received Holy Communion and returned to my place. All of a sudden, the Sacred Host began to grow on my tongue, becoming larger and thicker. It seemed to expand and then, suddenly, it came alive. Truly! strange though it must sound, I felt it as a living object. It must seem irreverently expressed; yet it may help people to form some idea of it when I say, "It resembled a living fish in its movements." I wanted to take it out of my mouth in order to see what it was; but of course, reverence prevented me from doing so.

As may be imagined, I got a terrible shock — it was awful! Never having experienced anything alike, I could not make out what was happening to me.

But at the same time a completely different perception arose in me, something so delightful. I may well say, something heavenly. It was a state such as I had never know. Then suddenly I heard,

"Be not afraid...I am the Lord, your Creator...the Lord Jesus Christ...The Giver of Life." (The dots indicate a silence.)

"Just as I live in you now, I want to and shall live among all nations."

After this the Sacred Host began to grow smaller and thinner; it resumed its usual form and I was able to consume it. Subsequently, I did not go to church for a whole week — excepting Sunday, of course — in order to check up on myself. Nothing out of the ordinary took place.

9th September, 1959

However, on September 9th I had the very same experience again and at the end I was told: "Do pass this on."

Since then, it has not happened again, although I have been to Holy Communion daily.

11th October, 1959

Today, however, October 11, 1959, it was repeated. The same experience, the same extra-ordinary state. Today the words were, "I am your Lord, your Creator...the Lord Jesus Christ...the Giver of Life...Fear nothing. Through the Will of the Father and the power of the Giver of Life, I shall and will dwell among all nations, just as I now dwell in you...Do understand the Daily Wonder. Do what She, who was sent by Me — 'the Lady of All Nations' — has told you to do...*Pass this on.*"

Then the Sacred Host decreased in size; I felt it dissolve on my tongue, becoming smaller and smaller, until nothing solid was left to consume. Only a liquid remained, which had a wonderful kind of taste, not to be compared with anything else.

18th October, 1959

As I walked back from the Communion rails, it seemed as though the Sacred Host was no longer on my tongue. Instead, I felt as if flows of water were entering my mouth. They kept streaming, I cannot express it otherwise. It had a very wonderful taste, wholly unknown to us. An exceptional state came over me and I heard, "I am the living Water. Warn My apostles, so that errors may be *obviated.*"

All the while, fresh water seemed to be flowing through my mouth. This lasted for a considerable time.

31st January, 1960

When I had received Holy Communion and was back at my place, it was all at once as though the muscles of my whole body began to pull and contract, which caused me excruciating pains. Suddenly, the sweat of death seemed to settle on my brow. It became ice-cold and I was ready to swoon.

I knew, however, that in reality I was not ill. Strangely enough, I was conscious of that! I remained sitting quietly, holding my hands before my eyes and of a sudden a most wonderful state came over me, such as I had experienced a few times before. It was as though I was being lifted up and floated somewhere. Then for a good while I remained wrapped in a heavenly state (if I may be permitted to say so).

When everything had gone, the Sacred Host was still unconsumed on my tongue.

25th March, 1960, Annunciation Day

During Holy Communion the Sacred Host suddenly broke into very small crumbs upon my tongue. All at once I heard, "I am the Seed, which was plunged into *Her* womb."

Upon this, the crumbs assumed a delicious taste and became fluid. Then I heard,

"I am the living Water."

Then I was startled by a violent, burning sensation on my tongue and I heard,

"Fear not. I am the eternal Fire that was kindled in *Her* womb for all nations."

Then the Sacred Host dissolved on my tongue.

31st May, 1960, Queenship of Our Lady

When I went to Holy Communion, I heard,

"I am the Lord, your Creator, the Risen Lord, the True Wisdom."

Then the Sacred Host became alive on my tongue and I heard, "I am the Fish; *you* are the salt of the earth. I am the living Water." (At this, flows of fresh water, with an exceptionally delicious taste, began pouring through my mouth.)

"I am the living Manna." (Now that water changed back into the Sacred Host.)

Then all at once the Sacred Host began to burn so violently on my tongue, that it seemed as if the latter would be consumed by a fire within. I got a shock and heard, "Fear nothing. I am the Fire that was kindled in the womb of the Lady. You, priests, do not let this fire go out; but carry it with you in your hearts, in your hands and on your lips, so that it may continue to burn and live among all nations. For they must all attain eternal life.

"Pass this on; the signs have been given. Do what the Lady told you to do."

Thus all at once the Sacred Host was back in its usual form on my tongue; and I consumed it.

One the same day, at 3:15 in the afternoon, I suddenly saw the light on the "Wandelweg"; but after a few minutes it vanished again.

30th October, 1960, Feast of Christ the King

When I went to Holy Communion, I felt the Sacred Host fall upon my tongue in three layers. From my palate one host at a time fell on my tongue and became one with the other. When that was over, the Sacred Host became very thick and large again and began to move, as I had experienced several times before.

All at once the Sacred Host dissolved and I tasted flows of delicious water. Then, suddenly, everything had gone. I heard no words.

15th January, 1961

When I went to Holy Communion and the Sacred Host became alive again on my tongue, I heard the words, "It is I...the living Christ...the Substance...I am present in the Bread, which you, priests, should distribute among all nations — and the Kingdom of God is in your midst."

26th February, 1961

Today I experienced the very same things as on January 15th. Precisely the same words were spoken. In addition, however, I heard at the end, "Pass this on."

25th March, 1961, Annunciation Day

At Communion everything proceeded again as related above. The Sacred Host fell as it were in three layers upon my tongue, where they joined into one and became alive. Subsequently, it melted into a delicious water. Then I heard,

"Walk along the way I have shown you."

"May peace be with you!"

And suddenly everything had gone.

It was childish, I know, but I could not help weeping, as all at once I felt such a dreadful void and loneliness encompass me, exactly as on the occasion of the Lady's last visit, only much worse.

31st May, 1962

On my way to Holy Communion I saw the light upon the altar. It stayed for a while and then disappeared again.

31st May, 1962

As I went to Holy Communion, the Sacred Host suddenly began to move and later changed into flows of water in my mouth. The light too, was present during that time. There was no message. Afterwards, everything went back to normal.

23rd May, 1963, Ascension Day

During Holy Communion I heard, not with my ears but interiorly, "Hold yourself in readiness for May 31st."

31st May, 1963

After Holy Communion, when I had gone back to my place, the Sacred Host all at once began to move again and I also heard a word (not with my ears). The word was "Transubstantiation..."and upon this the Sacred Host began to be active again on my tongue to a greater extent that ever before. Suddenly I heard, "I wanted to give them another chance."

After this, I saw (not with my eyes, as formerly) lips with a finger across and I heard,

"Do not tell anybody before it has happened..." Here the voice ceased for a moment, after which I heard, "Montini."

Then I tasted flows of water and the Sacred Host had gone.

31st May, 1964

While receiving Holy Communion, I heard,

"Go and speak with your Bishop."

I got a shock and said inwardly, "Oh! he won' t believe me in any case!" The voice repeated with urgency, "Go and speak with him." It sounded like a command. The Sacred Host became active again on my tongue. Only at the end of Holy Mass it melted away to a delicious liquid.

31st May, 1965

During Holy Communion the Sacred Host became active again on my tongue. I saw a pair of lips with a finger across. The finger made the sign of the Cross at those lips. Then I heard the voice say, "Thus it is all right."

There was a pause and after that I heard,

"Go to Pope Paul and tell him in the name of 'the Lady of All Nations:'

"This is the last warning before the end of the Council. The Church of Rome is in danger of a schism.

"Warn your priests. Let them put a stop to those *false* theories about the Eucharist, sacraments, doctrine, priesthood, marriage and family-planning. They are being led astray by the spirit of untruth — by Satan — and confused by the ideas of modernism. Divine teaching and laws are valid for all time and newly applicable to every period.

"Keep the primacy in your own hands. Grasp the meaning of these my words: the Church of Rome must remain the Church of Rome.

"Do what the Lord has demanded of you—in sending Me, the Lady or Mother of All Nations. You are the Pope who has been selected for this work. Let the nations say the prayer before My picture and the Holy Spirit will come! A Church or a people without a Mother is like a body without a soul.

"This period is now coming at an end."

There followed a pause after which I heard, "Go and take the following message to your Bishop in person: give back to the faithful their devotion to 'the Lady of All Nations' and grant permission for the building of the church I have shown."

Then the finger was withdrawn from the lips and the whole vision vanished from my eyes. Then again I heard, "Listen well and hand this on to your Bishop: the time is now at hand. Tell your pastors to remain united in 'doctrine.' —This is the last warning from the Lord."

There was a pause and then the voice said very slowly and softly,

"The time is *now* at hand."

(During the entire communication the Sacred Host remained active on my tongue. A feeling of great sadness came over me and I also noticed that all this was said with emphasis and that the voice sounded very sad.)

31st May, 1966

When I went to Holy Communion, I suddenly saw a light preceding me right up to the chalice. The priest was not standing in the light. When I turned round to go back to my place, the light went ahead of me and stayed around me for a considerable while, until the Sacred Host was consumed. In the meantime, I was twice given the following impression: "Thus it is all right."

19th June, 1966

When I entered the chapel in the Rue du Bac, Paris, a strange emotion came over me, such as I had never before experienced on visiting any church. I could not tell what it was, so much did it hold me captive. We participated in Holy Mass and I went to Holy Communion. When I got back to my place, the Sacred Host began to move again on my tongue and I quite distinctly heard the voice say (inwardly), "Do you now see the way I wanted? This is why I said, 'Thus it is all right.'" (I had heard this on May 31, 1966). Then the voice ceased for a moment, after which I heard, "So be it!"

During this message I was deeply moved. The light disappeared only when Holy Mass was over.

31st May, 1967

During Consecration I suddenly saw a light coming from the chalice. The priest was as if in the shade, standing in the background. When I went to Holy Communion and returned to my place, the Sacred Host began to move on my tongue and I heard the voice of the Lady say, "You have now met the Lord. You will not hear my voice again.

"I have promised to come back in private, for the priests and for the Church. Now I say: priests and religious, return to your *true* (the Lady stressed the word) vocation, to the call of the Lord.

"And to the Church, the Community, I say: take the picture back to the city and the place the Lord has appointed for it. Speak to your Bishop. It is high time!"

Now a terrifyingly evil pressure was laid on me and the kneeler seemed to collapse under my weight. I saw the world lying before me and felt a fearful danger threatening it.—Everything was as black as pitch. I heard the voice say,

"This is My last warning to you. I may yet save the world." Then the voice was silent for a moment, after which it resumed with emphasis,

"From now on My words shall cease."

Then I heard the Lady say a totally foreign word; like a cry it reached my ears. I do not know how to spell it; it seemed Jewish or Hebrew to me, with a very strong guttural sound: "Hoerach!" or "Gurach!"

I said to myself, "What is this I hear now? What does it mean?" And then the voice said,

"The Spirit will come. The contact will remain."

And then the light slowly faded away.

31st May, 1968

While I received Holy Communion, I saw the "light" coming again and then all at once I saw a large black Cross standing before me. That Cross moved farther and farther away from me and finally stood still in the distance. Then from the right side a great beam of light fell a-slant upon that Cross. The beam was so broad and powerful that it rendered the Cross invisible. Afterwards, the light disappeared. I heard no words. A heavenly feeling came over me and I had a strong realization of the Lord's presence.

31st May, 1969

On that day I was in Paris. In the church in the Rue du Bac I saw the light again while receiving Holy Communion and was given a very realistic perception of the Lord's presence. Then the following words impressed themselves very strongly upon me, though they were not uttered:

"What began here, will be continued by 'the Lady of All Nations.'"

Then I saw a group of people and it was as if I saw more and more groups appearing with a priest in every group. After all these experiences, the light very slowly faded away.

25th March, 1970

When Communion began, I suddenly saw the light settle above the altar. The light was not as I had usually seen it. It was different; and I heard inwardly: "The light is overshadowed." I do not know what this means. When I had received Holy Communion and returned to my place, I once again had a strong impression that "The Lord" was close by and in me. At the same moment, the light changed. It was exceedingly bright and more beautiful than ever before. Toward the end of Holy Mass, the light very slowly went away.

About 5 o' clock, looking from our window facing Kennedy-Lane, we saw a procession moving towards the place where the Lady's church is to be built. These were the people who had come to the Congres Building of the RAI in order to commemorate the 25th anniversary of the Lady's first apparition.

Within a few minutes of lively conversation with my sisters, I suddenly saw the light descending over the whole area and the people. It was as if heaven had opened. At that moment, I heard the voice of the Lady.

I thought, "That's impossible!," for the Lady had told me that Her words would cease." So I was exceedingly moved to hear Her voice again. Has She perhaps made an exception for this celebration? Unfortunately, I did not see Her. She spoke more quickly than usual and from emotion I did not repeat Her words aloud.

The Lady said, "You have met 'the Lord' again today; and today you may once more hear My voice."

She paused for a moment and then the voice continued, "I had wanted to bring an important and joyous message.—However, they have not listened."

Then I saw streams flooding over the ground. It looked like a raging sea. I heard, "The waves of degeneration, disaster and war, are engulfing the world ever more. Do not let yourselves be swept away by the flood-tides of spiritual confusion."

"Apostles of the Lord, remain faithful to your divine calling!"

The Lady again waited a little and then said in a very sad tone, "And you, poor souls that have lost your way, come back."

Then all was quiet and I saw the light becoming greater, more powerful and splendid. I heard the Lady say, "The hour is near. You, child, have acted well, very well; just as We wished. Fear nothing. Tell this to your Bishop." The light slowly faded away. I heard the voice as if coming from afar, saying, "Farewell."

31st May, 1970, Feast of Corpus Christi and the Queenship of Our Lady

During Holy Mass I had the following experience: Shortly before the Consecration I saw a large, black plane.

The plane formed itself into a big, black Cross. Then within this black Cross appeared a smaller, narrower and shining Cross that sparkled on all sides. This Cross, ablaze in the midst of the black Cross, shone so brightly, that the big Cross became wholly bathed in its light.

During the Consecration I saw the chalice that was being raised, encircled by a halo of brilliant light. From out of the chalice emerged, in horizontal position, a "Spiritualized, Sacred Host." This Sacred Host was translucent. After that the Sacred Host came to rest above the chalice in a vertical position.

I discerned a difference between the Host that was still lying in front of the priest, and the "Spiritualized, Sacred Host." This latter irradiated such splendour in all directions that it hurt my eyes.

Then the priest took the Host that lay before him and held it up. I saw the Spiritualized Sacred Host combine with the Host the priest was holding up and with it form one blazing light. This was a most resplendent sight — words cannot suffice for adequate comment.

The next thing I saw was that the light that shone round about the chalice and the priest, was tending in the direction of the spot (in our room) where the Lady had always appeared. Then the two lights became *one*. For, in the meantime, the light that always accompanied the Lady, had also entered the room. The whole room was now one ocean of light.

The chalice meanwhile stood on the altar and I now saw that blood was streaming out of it. At the same time I heard the words,

"They have reviled Me again."

"They have nailed Me to the Cross anew."

"Make atonement."

The light stayed in the room all the time. Then it looked as if the light was being parted and presently I saw the priest, ready to distribute Holy Communion.

When I had received Our Lord, I heard a sentence in an utterly strange tongue. I asked, "What does it mean?" and heard the answer, — "I AM THAT I AM."

It was not the voice of the Lady. I did not get the sense of this saying.

After a pause the voice said, "Make this message known to the whole world."

To this it added, as a command,

"Lead the Rosary this afternoon."

Then the light slowly vanished and I could see my surroundings again.

POSTSCRIPT

In this booklet, *The Messages of the Lady of All Nations,* the following statements are lacking because of the interpretation of my then Spiritual Director, Father J. Frehe O.P.

The Message of April 21, 1945, is missing

"And Israel will rise again."

The Lady said this after showing to me the Exodus from Egypt and the image of Cain and Abel.

31st May, 1956

In the Message of that day the Lady made the sign of the cross with Her thumb on Her lips and said:

"Don' t repeat this."

Then I heard:

"Tell the Sacristan to the Holy Father that he should indicate to him that 'Celibacy still is the great strength of the Church.'"
(This was said with emphasis).
"...There are people who wish this changed. But this should happen only in very exceptional circumstances. Tell this to the Holy Father. He will understand Me."

31st May, 1957

At the first pause in the Message the Lady made a cross with Her thumb at Her lips and said:

"Go to the Holy Father and tell him everything. Ask for his blessing on the Prayer. Ask for the Dogma."

I inwardly answered:
"Ah, my Lady, how can you ask that! You know I can never get there."

The Lady answered gently:

"Through the Sacristan."

I did not know the meaning of the word "Sacristan" and I asked a priest. He explained to me: "He is the Sacristan to the Pope, but not an ordinary sexton, for he is a Monsignore."

At the last pause in the Message, again making a thumb-crossing at Her lips, the Lady said:

"Go to the Holy Father and tell him that I have said: the time has now arrived for the Dogma to be proclaimed. I shall come back privately at the time chosen by the Lord to assist the Church and the priests. Say that celibacy is endangered from within, but the Holy Father must always uphold it, notwithstanding all opposition."

As I shook my head and said that I did not dare tell this, the Lady said somewhat angrily:

"I order you to tell it."

So I nodded –yes–.

"If they do what I have said, I will assist the peoples (each individually, even the most primitive) and I shall be permitted to bring true peace."

These are the statements of April 21, 1945 and May 31, 1956 and 1957, not yet published in *The Messages of the Lady of All Nations.*

In those days when there was not yet any apparent opposition regarding celibacy, Father Frehe thought it better not to publish these texts. Now times have changed and there exists much opposition to the celibacy of the priesthood, so I think the time has come not only to publish these texts, but also to call for special attention to them.

– I.P.

REFERENCE INDEX

(numbers denote apparitions)

GOD-THREE PERSONS AND ONE SUBSTANCE

God 20, 29, 49
Yahweh 2
The Highest 7
Creator 37
Blessed Trinity 38
Father, Son and Holy Spirit 32, 39, 42, 45, 51
God, the Father 2
Father 28, 29, 31, 32, 33, 37, 38, 39, 41, 45, 47
Father and Son 31, 32, 33, 34, 38, 41
Son 24, 27, 28, 29, 30, 31, 32, 33, 35, 37
Son of the Father 27, 41
My Son 17
Son Jesus Christ 37
The interests of my Son 29, 30
✠ Sign 9, 16
Christ 3, 9, 16, 19, 25, 32, 35, 49
Jesus Christ 35, 37
Lord Jesus Christ 27, 37, 39ff, 50ff, 53
The Lord 43, 44, 46, 49
Our Lord 7
My Lord 47
Lord and Master 43ff, 38, 39, 43
Man-God 32, 43
Son of Man 28

SEEING THE MORAL DECLINE OF THE WORLD
(Satan still being the Prince)

AND THE PEOPLE BEING LED ASTRAY BY
FALSE PROPHETS AND BAD MOVEMENTS

Materialism 30, 42
Realism 16
Socialism (modern) 4, 45, 46
Swastika 5, 6
Crescent 14
Sickle and Hammer 5, 14

AND THE WORLD DEGENERATING
WITH CALAMITOUS EFFECTS

Degenerating world 21ff, 28, 32, 35, 37, 42, 43
Satanic World 49
Governments have resigned 23
Crises:
    economic 14, 17, 20, 25, 36, 37
    spiritual 25, 36
Heavy pressure, great oppression 44, 45
Period of falling away from Faith 29
A spirit undermining mankind 6, 23, 29, 35, 44
A chasm, a rent in the earth 14, 19
The world is being revolutionized 27
The world is tottering 5
Chaotic world 38
The world will sink lower and lower 20
The world will destroy itself 11, 18, 29
Lost without justice 5
The world would perish 5
Chaos 8, 15, 23
Anxiety 42
Pain and misery 14, 15, 22
Unrest 42
Tension 42
Doubt 15
Desolation 13
Despair 15
Disorder 15

AND THERE WILL BE STRUGGLES,
SPIRITUAL STRUGGLES

AND THERE WILL BE DISASTERS

AND SOME INDISPENSABLE VIRTUES
ARE LACKING IN THE WORLD

It is the Centre 27, 33
Christ carries His Cross alone 5, 8

SENT IN THIS TIME

In this time 4, 21, 25, 27, 29, 31ff, 38ff, 43, 44, 47, 50
This time is Our time 27, 30 ff, 38, 39, 41, 42, 43
Moving with the time 5, 27
It is a serious, anxious time 32, 38, 41, 44
No time to wait 30, 36, 38, 44
It is the time of the Holy Spirit 42

MIRIAM OR MARY

Miriam or Mary 1, 34, 36, 38, 41, 43, 45, 47, 49, 50
She is the Immaculate Conception 49
She has crushed the snake 35
The Handmaid of the Lord 38, 39, 41, 43, 44, 49
Mother 1, 31, 32, 37, 41, 43, 44, 45, 47, 49
Mother of the Lord Jesus Christ 47, 49
Mother of the Son of Man 30
Mother of the Apostles 43, 44
Mother of the Bishop 49
Lady with the Child 9, 10, 16
Woman behold thy son 35, 41, 43

TO MANKIND AND THE WHOLE WORLD

Men, mankind, people-almost every page
World-almost every page

AS THE LADY OF ALL NATIONS

mentioned more than 150 times-24ff

WHO ONCE WAS MARY

27, 29, 34, 37, 39, 41, 42, 50

UNDER THE TITLE OF CO-REDEMPTRIX, MEDIATRIX AND ADVOCATE

mentioned more than 50 times-31ff

FROM THE BEGINNING

38, 43, 49

WITH MESSAGES

Message 13, 19, 21, 27ff, 35, 38, 39, 42, 44, 45, 46
Messages 23, 42, 43, 45, 47

WHICH MUST BE CONVEYED BY A WEAK AND FEARFUL INSTRUMENT

Instrument 27, 29, 33, 35, 45, 46, 47, 50
She must listen well (attentively) 19, 22, 23, 27, 39, 43, 49, 55
She must watch well and listen 19, 23, 26, 30, 33, 38, 52
She represents mankind 5, 6
A cross (crucifix) is put (laid) in Her hand 2, 6, 14, 15, 17, 20
She must raise two fingers 5, 9, 16, 25
She must make (clench) a fist 6, 23, 25, 27
She gets pain in Her hands 4, 5, 11, 13, 14, 15, 20, 21
Pain in body and soul 6, 8, 14, 20, 23, 25, 27, 29, 30, 31, 32, 37
She is tired 6, 8, 9, 30
She is afraid, frightened, fearful, anxious 29, 31, 46, 49
She can help by saying the prayer 30, 40, 43, 51
She does not understand why she has been chosen 43
She feels weak in the face of the task 28
Nevertheless she has to pass on the messages 29, 31ff, 34, 36ff, 38, 41, 46, 49
She must not hesitate 32, 33, 36, 43, 44
Everybody must co-operate 17, 18, 19, 27, 34, 42, 43, 47

Those in authority must work 18, 19
They must do what the Lady says 24, 27

IN A BRIGHT LIGHT

3, 13, 27ff, 31, 34, 52, 53, 54

SHE HEARS THE VOICE OF A LADY
DRESSED ALL IN WHITE

Lady dressed in white 1, 5, 6, 13
The voice 3, 5, 6, 12, 14, 23, 28, 29, 50, 54

HER FIRST MESSAGE CONCERNS
A NEW PRAYER

Text of the prayer 27
To be said before the Cross 27
Nothing must be altered in it 29, 39, 41
Mary herself says the Prayer 27, 29, 32
The Prayer given in the country where Satan had reigned 47
Through an instrument from the country where peace was always desired 47
Given for the salvation of the world 38
For the conversion of the world 38
For the benefit of all nations 38
To be said by the seeress during Her daily life 38
The Prayer will remain until the end 44
It will be said in all churches 44
It must be said every day 28, 30, 31, 34

A PRAYER TO SAVE THE WORLD FROM
DEGENERATION, DISASTERS AND WAR

27, 31, 38, 43

HER SECOND MESSAGE CONCERNS
A NEW IMAGE
(which is dealt with numerous times)

HER THIRD MESSAGE CONCERNS THE WORLD-
WIDE SPREADING OF PRAYER AND PICTURE

HER FOURTH MESSAGE CONCERNS
THE LAST MARIAN DOGMA

THESE FOUR MESSAGES APPLY TO THE WHOLE
WORLD AS APPEARS FROM HER ACTIONS

She takes the globe in Her hand 11
She is concerned about the fleeing sheep along the globe 40
She changes the globe into a flat map 25
She shows how black and dark the situation is on the globe 5, 8

THE EXPRESSION ON HER FACE AND HER ATTITUDE SHOW HER GREAT AFFECTION TOWARDS THE WORLD

The Lady smiles 1, 3, 4, 5, 8, 9, 13, 20, 30, 32, 33, 34, 37, 46, 49, 50ff, 53
Her face brightens 13
She looks sad, very sad 4, 5, 24, 49, 50, 53
The caring mother 3, 27, 46
She gives Her blessing 35, 51
Compassionately 11, 25, 49
Dejectedly 10, 24
Encouragingly 5
Disapprovingly 25, 28, 29
A (very) serious face 6, 8, 49
Severe, stern 5, 8, 20
She shakes Her head 6, 7, 8, 9, 11, 17, 25, 28, 50, 53
Clenches Her fist 9
Angrily 37
Strikes the table with Her fist 25
Tears and sufferings 16, 27, 31, 32, 35
Clad in mourning 16
The sword thrust 32
Collapses and weeps bitterly 32

IN AND BETWEEN THESE FOUR MESSAGES THE LADY GIVES WARNINGS at almost every page, BUT AT THE SAME TIME PROMISES SUPPORT

20, 33, 36, 38, 44, 45, 46, 47, 49, 50, 51, 53, 55

SHE GIVES SIGNS

40, 43, 44, 45, 49

SHE WILL BRING THE TRUE PEACE, WHICH IS NOW LACKING IN THE WORLD

2, 6, 9, 12, 23, 30, 32ff, 38, 39, 41, 45ff, 50, 51

SHE WILL GRANT SPIRITUAL UNITY

Among the Churches 3, 4, 5, 6, 9, 11, 16, 20, 23, 24
Among the Christians 15, 35, 36, 39
In Europe 7, 20, 25
Among black and white 47, 51
Among the Nations 47, 51
In the families 24
Unity 47
Under the Cross 39
One in Jesus Christ 35
Ask the Lady in Amsterdam 46

FOR WHOM ARE THESE MESSAGES INTENDED?

The Pope 4ff, 7, 12, 15, 16, 19, 20, 23, 25, 27, 36, 38ff, 41, 43, 45, 54
The Holy Father 36, 43f, 45, 47, 49, 50, 51, 54
The Fighter 4, 36, 37, 39, 43, 44
The Supreme Pastor 55
Decree 19, 26
Encyclical letters 5, 23, 44
Doctrine and laws 19, 27, 37, 39
Changes 4, 5, 7, 19, 23f, 25, 27, 35, 40, 41, 42, 49
Vatican 5, 12, 21, 24, 27
St. Peter's 15, 16, 17, 19, 20, 22, 49
Urbi et Orbi 10, 23
Sacristan 44, 45, 46, 47, 49, 54, 55

WARNINGS TO OR FOR CONTINENTS, COUNTRIES AND NATIONS

ADDITIONAL ALPHABETICAL INDEX
(numbers denote apparitions)